T0181986

Lecture Notes in Computer Science 12995

More information about this subseries at https://link.springer.com/bookseries/7408

Ajay Katangur · Liang-Jie Zhang (Eds.)

Services Computing
– SCC 2021

18th International Conference
Held as Part of the Services Conference Federation, SCF 2021
Virtual Event, December 10–14, 2021
Proceedings

 Springer

Editors
Ajay Katangur
Missouri State University
Springfield, IL, USA

Liang-Jie Zhang ⓘ
Kingdee International Software Group
Co., Ltd.
Shenzhen, China

ISSN 0302-9743 ISSN 1611-3349 (electronic)
Lecture Notes in Computer Science
ISBN 978-3-030-96565-5 ISBN 978-3-030-96566-2 (eBook)
https://doi.org/10.1007/978-3-030-96566-2

LNCS Sublibrary: SL2 – Programming and Software Engineering

This Springer imprint is published by the registered company Springer Nature Switzerland AG
The registered company address is: Gewerbestrasse 11, 6330 Cham, Switzerland

Preface

Services account for a major part of the IT industry today. Companies increasingly like to focus on their core expertise area and use IT services to address all their peripheral needs. Services computing is a new science that aims to study and better understand the foundations of this highly popular industry. It covers the science and technology of leveraging computing and information technology to model, create, operate, and manage business services. The 2021 International Conference on Services Computing (SCC 2021) contributed to building the pillars of this important science and shaping the future of services computing.

SCC has been a prime international forum for both researchers and industry practitioners to exchange the latest fundamental advances in the state of the art and practice of business modeling, business consulting, solution creation, service delivery, and software architecture design, development, and deployment.

This volume presents the accepted papers for SCC 2021, held as a fully virtual conference during December 10–December 14, 2021. For SCC 2021, we accepted seven papers. Each paper was reviewed and by at least three independent members of the SCC 2021 international Program Committee. We are pleased to thank the authors whose submissions and participation made this conference possible. We also want to express our thanks to the Organizing Committee and Program Committee members for their dedication in helping to organize the conference and reviewing the submissions. We owe special thanks to the keynote speakers for their impressive speeches.

December 2021

Ajay Katangur
Liang-Jie Zhang

Organization

SCC 2021 General Chair

John Miller   University of Georgia, USA

SCC 2021 Program Chair

Ajay Katangur   Missouri State University, USA

Services Conference Federation (SCF 2021)

General Chairs

Wu Chou   Essenlix Corporation, USA
Calton Pu (Co-chair)   Georgia Tech, USA
Dimitrios Georgakopoulos   Swinburne University of Technology, Australia

Program Chairs

Liang-Jie Zhang   Kingdee International Software Group Co., Ltd.,
                                        China
Ali Arsanjani   Amazon Web Services, USA

CFO

Min Luo   Georgia Tech, USA

Industry Track Chairs

Awel Dico   Etihad Airways, UAE
Rajesh Subramanyan   Amazon Web Services, USA
Siva Kantamneni   Deloitte Consulting, USA

Industry Exhibit and International Affairs Chair

Zhixiong Chen   Mercy College, USA

Operations Committee

Jing Zeng   China Gridcom Co., Ltd., China
Yishuang Ning   Tsinghua University, China
Sheng He   Tsinghua University, China

Steering Committee

Calton Pu (Co-chair)   Georgia Tech, USA
Liang-Jie Zhang (Co-chair)   Kingdee International Software Group Co., Ltd.,
                                 China

SCC 2021 Program Committee

Sanjay Chaudhary   Ahmedabad University, India
Lizhen Cui   Shandong University, China
Kenneth Fletcher   University of Massachusetts Boston, USA
Pedro Furtado   University de Coimbra/CISUC, Portugal
Alfredo Goldman   USP, Brazil
Shigeru Hosono   Tokyo University of Technology, Japan
Shijun Liu   Shandong University, China
Markus Lumpe   Swinburne University of Technology, Australia
Xin Luo   Chongqing University, China
Marcio Oikawa   Federal University of ABC, Brazil
Fredy Humberto Rivera   Universidad Francisco de Paula Santander,
                         Colombia
Andre Luis Schwerz   Federal University of Technology Paraná, Brazil
Jun Shen   University of Wollongong, Australia
Yang Syu   National Taipei University of Education, Taiwan
Dingwen Tao   Washington State University, USA
Yunni Xia   Chongqing University, China
Yu-Bin Yang   Nanjing University, China
Muhammad Younas   Oxford Brookes University, UK

Conference Sponsor – Services Society

The Services Society (S2) is a non-profit professional organization that has been created to promote worldwide research and technical collaboration in services innovations among academia and industrial professionals. Its members are volunteers from industry and academia with common interests. S2 is registered in the USA as a "501(c) organization", which means that it is an American tax-exempt non-profit organization. S2 collaborates with other professional organizations to sponsor or co-sponsor conferences and to promote an effective services curriculum in colleges and universities. S2 initiates and promotes a "Services University" program worldwide to bridge the gap between industrial needs and university instruction.

The services sector accounted for 79.5% of the GDP of the USA in 2016. Hong Kong has one of the world's most service-oriented economies, with the services sector accounting for more than 90% of GDP. As such, the Services Society has formed 10 Special Interest Groups (SIGs) to support technology and domain specific professional activities:

- Special Interest Group on Web Services (SIG-WS)
- Special Interest Group on Services Computing (SIG-SC)
- Special Interest Group on Services Industry (SIG-SI)
- Special Interest Group on Big Data (SIG-BD)
- Special Interest Group on Cloud Computing (SIG-CLOUD)
- Special Interest Group on Artificial Intelligence (SIG-AI)
- Special Interest Group on Edge Computing (SIG-EC)
- Special Interest Group on Cognitive Computing (SIG-CC)
- Special Interest Group on Blockchain (SIG-BC)
- Special Interest Group on Internet of Things (SIG-IOT)

About the Services Conference Federation (SCF)

As the founding member of the Services Conference Federation (SCF), the First International Conference on Web Services (ICWS) was held in June 2003 in Las Vegas, USA. In addition, the First International Conference on Web Services - Europe 2003 (ICWS-Europe 2003) was held in Germany in October of the same year. In 2004, ICWS-Europe was changed to the European Conference on Web Services (ECOWS), which was held in Erfurt, Germany. The 19th edition in the conference series, SCF 2021, was held virtually over the Internet during December 10–14, 2021.

In the past 18 years, the ICWS community has expanded from Web engineering innovations to scientific research for the whole services industry. The service delivery platforms have expanded to mobile platforms, the Internet of Things (IoT), cloud computing, and edge computing. The services ecosystem has gradually been enabled, value added, and intelligence embedded through enabling technologies such as big data, artificial intelligence, and cognitive computing. In the coming years, transactions with multiple parties involved will be transformed by blockchain.

Based on the technology trends and best practices in the field, SCF will continue serving as the conference umbrella's code name for all services-related conferences. SCF 2021 defined the future of the New ABCDE (AI, Blockchain, Cloud, big Data, Everything is connected), which enable IoT and support the "5G for Services Era". SCF 2021 featured 10 collocated conferences all centered around the topic of "services", each focusing on exploring different themes (e.g. web-based services, cloud-based services, big data-based services, services innovation lifecycle, AI-driven ubiquitous services, blockchain-driven trust service-ecosystems, industry-specific services and applications, and emerging service-oriented technologies). The SCF 2021 members were as follows:

1. The 2021 International Conference on Web Services (ICWS 2021, http://icws.org/), which was the flagship conference for web-based services featuring web services modeling, development, publishing, discovery, composition, testing, adaptation, and delivery, as well as the latest API standards.
2. The 2021 International Conference on Cloud Computing (CLOUD 2021, http://the cloudcomputing.org/), which was the flagship conference for modeling, developing, publishing, monitoring, managing, and delivering XaaS (everything as a service) in the context of various types of cloud environments.
3. The 2021 International Conference on Big Data (BigData 2021, http://bigdataco ngress.org/), which focused on the scientific and engineering innovations of big data.
4. The 2021 International Conference on Services Computing (SCC 2021, http://the scc.org/), which was the flagship conference for the services innovation lifecycle including enterprise modeling, business consulting, solution creation, services orchestration, services optimization, services management, services marketing, and business process integration and management.

5. The 2021 International Conference on AI and Mobile Services (AIMS 2021, http://ai1000.org/), which addressed the science and technology of artificial intelligence and the development, publication, discovery, orchestration, invocation, testing, delivery, and certification of AI-enabled services and mobile applications.

6. The 2021 World Congress on Services (SERVICES 2021, http://servicescongress.org/), which put its focus on emerging service-oriented technologies and industry-specific services and solutions.

7. The 2021 International Conference on Cognitive Computing (ICCC 2021, http://thecognitivecomputing.org/), which put its focus on Sensing Intelligence (SI) as a Service (SIaaS), making a system listen, speak, see, smell, taste, understand, interact, and/or walk, in the context of scientific research and engineering solutions.

8. The 2021 International Conference on Internet of Things (ICIOT 2021, http://iciot.org/), which addressed the creation of IoT technologies and the development of IoT services.

9. The 2021 International Conference on Edge Computing (EDGE 2021, http://theedgecomputing.org/), which put its focus on the state of the art and practice of edge computing including, but not limited to, localized resource sharing, connections with the cloud, and 5G devices and applications.

10. The 2021 International Conference on Blockchain (ICBC 2021, http://blockchain1000.org/), which concentrated on blockchain-based services and enabling technologies.

Some of the highlights of SCF 2021 were as follows

- Bigger Platform: The 10 collocated conferences (SCF 2021) got sponsorship from the Services Society which is the world-leading not-for-profits organization (501 c(3)) dedicated to serving more than 30,000 services computing researchers and practitioners worldwide. A bigger platform means bigger opportunities for all volunteers, authors, and participants. In addition, Springer provided sponsorship for best paper awards and other professional activities. All 10 conference proceedings of SCF 2021 will be published by Springer and indexed in the ISI Conference Proceedings Citation Index (included in Web of Science), the Engineering Index EI (Compendex and Inspec databases), DBLP, Google Scholar, IO-Port, MathSciNet, Scopus, and ZBlMath.
- Brighter Future: While celebrating the 2021 version of ICWS, SCF 2021 highlighted the Fourth International Conference on Blockchain (ICBC 2021) to build the fundamental infrastructure for enabling secure and trusted services ecosystems. It will also lead our community members to create their own brighter future.
- Better Model: SCF 2021 continued to leverage the invented Conference Blockchain Model (CBM) to innovate the organizing practices for all 10 collocated conferences.

Contents

Rule-Based Extraction of Tuple-Based Service Demand from Natural Language-Based Software Requirement for Automated Service Composition

Yang Syu[1,2], Yu-Jen Tsao[2], and Chien-Min Wang[2(✉)]

[1] Department of Information Science, National Taipei University of Education, Taipei City,
Taiwan (R.O.C.)
yangsyu@mail.ntue.edu.tw
[2] Institute of Information Science, Academia Sinica, Taipei City, Taiwan (R.O.C.)
{yangsyu,as2435677,cmwang}@iis.sinica.edu.tw

Abstract. In recent years, automated service composition (ASC) has become popular and prevalent in software engineering and services computing. Nevertheless, although there are many existing research works on ASC, a number of problems and issues in this research area remain to be addressed. Based on our observations, one of the major problems and insufficiencies of current ASC approaches is that many of them accept and consider only tuple-based service requirements, whereas it is unrealistic to assume that all users of an ASC approach can express their service demands in this manner. To most service and software stakeholders, the most natural and best way to describe their requirements is to express them in natural language. Due to this difference in formations, most existing ASC approaches are useless or difficult to use for ordinary users. In this paper, we attempt to bridge this gap between the conventional descriptions of user requirements and the acceptable inputs of current ASC approaches by proposing and implementing a new approach. This approach uses natural language processing (NLP) technologies to obtain the required information from natural language-based requirement descriptions to generate tuple-based service demands for ASC approaches. Based on the part-of-speech and dependency information parsed and provided by an adopted NLP processor, we define a set of rules and preprocessing methods to extract the intended service requirement elements. Finally, with a real-world software description dataset, the developed system is fully tested and demonstrates accurate extraction performance.

Keywords: Service computing · Natural language processing · Software engineering · Service composition

1 Introduction

Currently, the demands for software applications and services are dramatically increasing. To develop systems that satisfy those requirements, the traditional approaches in

---

Y. Syu and Y.-J. Tsao—The co-first authors.

© Springer Nature Switzerland AG 2022
A. Katangur and L.-J. Zhang (Eds.): SCC 2021, LNCS 12995, pp. 1–17, 2022.
https://doi.org/10.1007/978-3-030-96566-2_1

software engineering are costly and time-consuming. Thus, to reduce the cost and time for building intended software applications and systems, a principle called *reuse* has been widely adopted in both practice and research. Its idea is as follows: instead of developing and programming from scratch, use existing resources such as well developed, fully tested software components as much as possible. Currently, there are various development approaches and engineering techniques that practice this principle; among them, a method called service composition (SC) is quite popular and prevalent in practice. In SC, developers and engineers generate or produce a composite service to satisfy a received software demand by swiftly composing existing component services available on the Internet or in certain service repositories. Thus, the cost and time of producing an intended software product can be much lower than those of a traditional way. Although SC is comparatively more efficient, researchers in academia want to further improve it and attempt to minimize its working effort. Thus, researchers working on this goal concentrate on automating the entire composition process. This research area and such composition have been named automated service composition (ASC). A cost comparison between SC and ASC can be found in [1].

Due to its numerous advantages, ASC has been widely considered and well studied for many years, and it has accumulated a large number of works and literature. However, although there are many ASC approaches in research, an obstacle between them and their practical usage is that most of them only accept and take tuple-based service demands as the input [2]. Meanwhile, in most real-world situations, software requesters express their requirements in natural language instead of in a specific format [3] (in addition, in [4–6], the authors explain why natural language is the best way to express service demands). Considering these two facts, there is an obvious gap between the conventional formation of software requirements and the restricted inputs of current ASC approaches. This gap hampers the practical usability of existing ASC research and decreases the degree of automation of ASC approaches because natural language software requirements must be manually transformed into tuple-based service demands beforehand.

To address the problem and fill the gap, we propose an approach to automatically extract the intended information from natural language-based requirement descriptions to form tuple-based service demands for ASC approaches without any human intervention or transformation. Overall, we perform a two-stage study to develop an approach for the problem. First, since the most natural and convenient form of expressing software requirements is natural language, the first stage of our study employs an NLP processor called CoreNLP [7], which was developed and maintained by the Stanford NLP Group and has been widely considered the most powerful and precise NLP processor [8], to analyze and parse the sentences in human-written requirement descriptions. CoreNLP provides several different types of linguistic information of the targeted text for its users. In this study, we consider two of them: the part-of-speech of the words in the processed sentences and the disparate dependencies between the words. In addition, we use tokenization and coreference resolution offered by the processor to perform our preprocessing. Afterwards, based on the obtained linguistic information, the second stage of our study involves developing and using a set of self-defined preprocessing methods and NLP rules to generate the desired tuple-based service demands. As explained in Sect. 3, the preprocessing methods and NLP rules are specifically designed for our NLP application (i.e., to gain tuple-based requirement elements). As surveyed in [2], most existing ASC approaches adopt IOPE tuples (i.e., input, output, preconditioning, and postconditioning), which are the essential information for a (intended) service, as their acceptable or required approach input. In this paper, however, as the first study of this research topic, we consider input and output tuples, which are the most common and basic tuples in current ASC research [2].

Finally, to evaluate our approach and the implemented system, we employ a set of real-world software requirement descriptions as our experimental dataset and annotate them with their corresponding IO tuples, which makes them our ground truth for experimentation. Subsequently, we run the developed system on the dataset and present its performance in terms of several quantitative measures, including the accuracy, recall, precision, and F1 score. The experimental results demonstrate that the proposed approach can accurately identify and retrieve intended information to generate tuple-based service requirements.

The remainder of this paper is organized as follows. First, we describe our entire research process in Sect. 2. Subsequently, Sect. 3 elaborates the proposed approach, including its basic foundation, preprocessing, and rule-based extraction. Section 4 demonstrates the experimentation of the developed approach, including a discussion of the empirical results. Finally, we conclude this paper in Sect. 5 with a description of future work.

2 Research Process

In this section, we concisely depict how we perform this study. The purpose of this study is to have an NLP-based approach to obtain requirement descriptions in an intended format. More specifically, the approach takes natural language-based requirement descriptions as the input. After an internal process, it generates tuple-based service demands as the output, which can be taken and accepted by existing ASC approaches as the input of their composition task.

To the best of our knowledge, the targeted problem has never been considered and addressed before. Thus, there is no collection of human service requirement descriptions or text available. Therefore, to have materials to define and evaluate our NLP-based processing and extraction, we first seek human-written ASC requests in the ASC literature. However, only a dozen requests (sentences) can be found, which are far from the intended quantity and diversity. Thus, in this study, we adopt *Leetcode* [9], which contains many functional descriptions, each of which implicates the input and output of a wanted software component and is similar to service requirements, as our main source of natural language-based service demands. Afterwards, we manually annotate these human descriptions with their corresponding IO tuples to make and use them as our ground-truth dataset for subsequent approach development and quantitative evaluation. With the dataset, which is our analyzable parsing target, the next step is to devise our approach. Since the expected and assumed requirement descriptions are human-written text, we must use modern NLP technology. Consequently, the basis of our approach and implemented system is a powerful natural language processing tool/processor called CoreNLP. With the parsed linguistic information and the functionalities of the NLP processor, we can realize the structures of human requirement descriptions and the relationships between their elements (e.g., sentences and words) and use this understanding to design our approach. As a result, the devised approach comprises two different stages: preprocessing and rule-based extraction, which are elaborated in Sect. 3. Finally, with the collected and annotated real-world dataset and the implemented system, we evaluate and test the proposed approach by feeding unseen requirement sentences to the system, comparing the outcomes of the system (i.e., the identified tuples) with their corresponding answers (the annotated tuples), and finally calculating the quantitative performance of the system, as presented in Sect. 4.

3   Approach

The devised approach is exhaustively explained in this section. First, in Sect. 3.1, we briefly introduce the NLP techniques and acquired information (i.e., part-of-speech tagging and dependency parsing) in our approach. Then, we exemplify how the developed approach can employ these tagging and parsing results to obtain the intended information. Afterwards, a graphical overview of the proposed approach is demonstrated in the last part of this section. Regarding the proposed approach, it has been found that similar to many other NLP applications and solutions, performing some preprocessing steps on the targeted text before performing our rule-based extraction can result in superior effectiveness and higher precision. Thus, the devised approach comprises these two disparate stages, as elaborated in Sects. 3.2 and 3.3, respectively.

3.1   Natural Language Processing and the Two-Stage Approach

This study adopts CoreNLP as our underlying NLP processor, which provides several types of linguistic information and functionalities for its users, such as tokenization, coreference resolution, named entity recognition, and open information extraction [7]. As explained in Sect. 3.2, the preprocessing (first) stage of the proposed approach relies on tokenization and coreference resolutions offered by CoreNLP to generate the tokens of processed sentences and replace the pronouns that appear in a sentence with their original subjects. Afterwards, in the rule-based extraction (i.e., the second stage), the devised approach employs part-of-speech (PoS) tagging and dependency parsing, which offer information to realize the basic properties (PoSs) and relationships (dependencies) of the elements (words) of a processed text. With this understanding (i.e., tagging and parsing results) and a set of designed extraction rules, we can obtain intended elements and information from human requirement descriptions. In different NLP applications, PoS and dependencies are the two most basic and widely used types of linguistic information to design their solutions.

As a demonstration and introduction, Fig. 1 illustrates the results of PoS tagging and dependency parsing on a simple service description collected from the ASC literature. First, as shown in Fig. 1, PoS tagging attaches each word (token) in the description with its recognized part-of-speech tag. For example, CoreNLP considers *Sa*, *returns*, *the*, and *blood* as a singular proper noun (NNP), third-person singular present verb (VBZ),

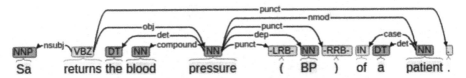

Fig. 1. Results of PoS tagging and dependency parsing for a service description.

determiner (DT), and singular/mass noun (NN) of the sentence. Meanwhile, the dependency parsing identifies the correct type of dependency between two correlated words (tokens). For example, within the example sentence, a nominal subject (nsubj) dependency between *Sa* and *returns*, object (obj) dependency between *returns* and *pressure*, and punctuation (punct) dependency between *returns* and the period of the sentence are identified by the NLP processor. A detailed definition of CoreNLP PoS tags and dependency types can be found in [10].

Based on accurately annotated PoS and dependency information, we can develop proper extraction rules to obtain the intended component and required information. As an example, in Fig. 1, *Sa* is a service name (NNP), and the sentence contains keyword *returns* (VBZ), which indicates that the service will generate something as its execution outcome for its consumers. Hence, it is reasonable to consider that the element following the keyword *returns* is the output component of this service (i.e., Output tuple). With this consideration and based on the CoreNLP parsing result, we can employ object dependency to obtain the element returned from the service. In this case, with this preliminary rule, *pressure* is retrieved, since there is an object dependency (obj) between *returns* (VBZ) and *pressures* (NN). Moreover, a possibility that must be considered and addressed is that the retrieved noun can be a compound noun. For this possibility, we can check the existence of a compound dependency (compound) associated with the retrieved noun (*pressure*) and, if so, use it to obtain the complete noun. Consequently, in our example, we can recover the compound noun *blood pressure*. Furthermore, another possibility is the possession of a noun; thus, we must add and revise the defined rule to cover and handle this situation. For our example, possession can be resolved through an improved extraction rule that considers the nominal modifier (nmod) dependency between *pressure* (NN) and *patient* (NN). Eventually, with a set of properly designed rules and reliable NLP results, the intended tuple can be extracted (in this case, the output tuple of the example service *patient blood pressure*).

A graphical overview of the proposed approach is presented in Fig. 2. Externally, the devised approach takes human-written requirement descriptions as running materials, and the processing outcome of the approach will be their corresponding tuple-based service demands. Internally, as mentioned, the approach consists of two different stages: preprocessing and rule-based extraction. In this study, we consider the two most basic and common service tuples (i.e., input and output). Based on our observation of the collected real-world software requirement descriptions, information regarding IO tuples mostly follows by some keywords such as *given, input, return,* and *output*. Thus, our extraction rules are designed based on these keywords, and a restriction on the approach input is the inclusion of at least one of these keywords.

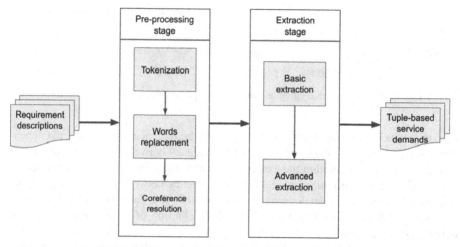

Fig. 2. Illustration of the developed two-stage approach.

3.2 Pre-processing

In this preprocessing stage, to the received requirement descriptions, we first perform tokenization to obtain correct NLP annotating results and subsequently perform coreference resolution for more specific tuple-based service elements. As the first step of the devised approach, we use CoreNLP to tokenize the targeted descriptions and subsequently replace some tokens that can cause incorrect NLP processing results, such as strange service names and semicolons. For example, on the left side of Fig. 3, an abbreviation (*findRestaurant*) cascadingly results in wrong NLP annotating outcomes (e.g., *returns*, which should be a VBZ, has been incorrectly identified as NNS, which is a type of noun). As shown in the right part of Fig. 3, this issue can be solved by substituting that service name with a normal service code (in this case, *Service_#*). Finally, the tokens that had been replaced are stored in an array to be later retrieved.

Fig. 3. Result of the PoS tagging and dependency parsing after replacing tokens.

The purpose of the second preprocessing step is to improve the quality and clarity of our extraction results, which we demonstrate using a real case in Fig. 4. On the left-hand side of Fig. 4 (the bottom part shows the extraction results), the possession/subject (*its*) of the second extracted element (*rating*) is unclear without reviewing the original sentence. Thus, in this step, we employ the coreference resolution provided by CoreNLP to retrieve coreferential words such as pronouns and common nouns, so that the following extraction stage can work on more specific materials and generate clearer outcomes, as the results show in the bottom right part of Fig. 4 (i.e., *closest restaurant rating*).

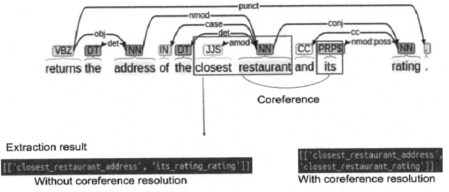

Fig. 4. An example of extraction results with and without coreference resolution.

3.3 Rule-Based Extraction

Our extraction rules are developed based on an exhaustive analysis and observation of the grammatical structures and sentence patterns of the collected human-written requirement descriptions. As a result, we have several major findings that are common in the reviewed text (i.e., the common writing and expressive conventions), and these findings are the basis of the definition of our extraction rules. Below, we first introduce the rules developed for basic extraction (i.e., basic extraction rules), followed by a set of advanced rules to acquire more detailed information and handle vague NLP annotating results (advanced extraction rules).

Basic Extraction Rules

The process of our basic extraction is demonstrated in Fig. 5 and explained in detail below. First, as the foundation of our extraction, the first two major findings are that (1) in most descriptions, the intended information (i.e., the input/output elements of a described service/software component) is associated with specific verbs (i.e., keywords such as *return, given,* and *output*), and (2) the meaning of a verb keyword can be used to determine and categorize the class of the extracted information (i.e., to which tuple it belongs). With these two basic facts, we first define a set of keywords for input and output tuples (i.e., *InputKeywordsSet* and *OutputKeywordsSet* in *Algorithm 1*), and we use them as an anchor in a targeted description for subsequent processing.

At the beginning of the process (i.e., the first step in Fig. 5), for a received requirement description, the implemented system first searches for the appearance of a defined keyword (i.e., an anchor). If the keyword appears, the system determines to which service tuple this keyword belongs (from which keyword set it originates). Afterwards,

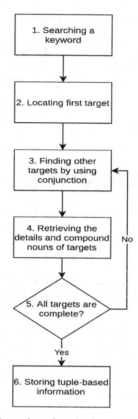

Fig. 5. Illustration of our basic extraction process.

based on a set of selected NLP dependencies, including *obj*, *iobj* (indirect object), and *case* (case-marking), a target element can be retrieved (the second step in the process). As an instance, *the service returns* (anchor) *price* (target). The details of this procedure are shown in Algorithm 1.

Next, considering the possibility that service descriptive elements could be multiple (e.g., *the service consumes temperature, number of people, and location as input*), we must consider this finding. Here, in the third step of the process, the conjunction dependencies (*conj*) associated with the originally anchored target (*temperature*) are employed to retrieve all other targets in a sentence (*people and location*), as described in Algorithm 2. Afterwards, the current processing results are stored and sent to Algorithm 3 and Algorithm 4 for further handling and retrieval (the fourth and fifth steps in Fig. 5).

Algorithm 1: Locate a initial target word and store information

---

Input: Service requirement descriptions with keywords

1 Create global vector information array;
2 Create I, O empty arrays;
3 **for** *token ∈ sentence* **do**
4   **if** *token ∈ InputKeywordsSet* **then**
5   Find token-related relations and use these relations such as obj to locate initial target word;
6   Send to Algorithm 2 to find words connected by conjunctions;
7   Append returned information in array I;
8   **end**
9   **else if** *token ∈ OutputKeywordsSet* **then**
10   Find token-related relations and use these relations such as obj to locate initial target word;
11   Send to Algorithm 2 to find words connected by conjunctions;
12   Append returned information in array O;
13   **end**
14 **end**

Algorithm 2: Find words connected by conjunctions

Input: initial target token index, tokens, words' dependencies, PoS tagging

1 Create empty array TargetWords;
2 Append index of initial target token into TargetWords;
3 Create len = 1 represent length of TargetWords;
4 Create index = 0;
5 **while** *len! = index* **do**
6   CurrentWord = *TargetWords*[*index*];
7   **for** *dep in words' dependencies* **do**
8   **if** *Find word connected to CurrentWord by conjunction* **then**
9   Append to TargetWords;
10   **end**
11   **end**
12   index = index + 1;
13   len = length of TargetWords;
14 **end**
15 Send TargetWords to Algorithm 3. to find details information;

Both Algorithm 3 and Algorithm 4 are designed to restore (complete) the details of the previously retrieved targets, but they are for two different cases. First, Algorithm 3 is dedicated to handling sentences that contain compound nouns or adjectival modifiers. For example, for a description of *the service returns credit card information*, the outcome of Algorithm 2 will be only the anchored target *information*; however, after running

Algorithm 3, the entire compound noun *credit card information* can be retrieved based on the NLP compound dependencies (*compound*) chained between them (there is a compound dependency between *information* and *card* and between *card* and *credit*, respectively).

Algorithm 3: Recover compound word

Input: index of target token, words' dependencies, tokens
Output: Compound word

1 Create empty array CompoundWord;
2 **for** $dep \in$ *words' dependencies* **do**
3   **if** *Words connected to target token by Compound relation* **then**
4   *Append to CompoundWord;*
5   *PreviousWord = Previous word of target token;*
6        $i = 0;$
7   **while** $i <$ *length of words' dependencies* **do**
8   **if** *Words connected to PreviousWord by Compound relation* **then**
9   *Append to CompoundWord;*
10   *PreviousWord = Previous word of current token;*
11              $i = 0;$
12   **end**
13           $i = i + 1;$
14   **end**
15   **end**
16   **else if** *Modifiers connected to target token* **then**
17   *Append to CompoundWord;*
18   **end**
19 **end**
20 *Use CompoundWord to recover a word and return it;*

Another finding is that the retrieved (compound) targets can have descriptive details connected with them using prepositions such as *for, from*, and *of*. For example, for the sentence *the service returns the blood pressure of this person, blood pressure* will be the processing result after running Algorithms 1, 2, and 3, for the Output tuple of the service; however, its possessive information *this person* is missing. Thus, Algorithm 4 is designed to address this situation using the nominal modifier dependency (*nmod*) to obtain basic descriptive details for targets (more detailed information will be retrieved by applying advance extraction rules, which are introduced in next section). In addition, this detailed information is sent to be processed by Algorithm 3 if it contains compound nouns (e.g., *this person*).

Algorithm 4: Find details of words

Input: target token, words' dependency, tokens, PoS tagging

1 Create a global vector information array;

2 TargetIndex = -1;

3 k = 1;

4 information = result of input target token to Algorithm 3;

5 **for** *dep* ∈ *words' dependencies* **do**

6   **if** *dep = nmod and connect to target token* **then**

7 | TargetIndex = token connect to target token;

8   **end**

9   **else if** *dep = case and connect to target token and related to prepositions of or for or from* **then**

10 | k = 0;

11   **end**

12   **else if** *other relations such as dep = nmod : poss that connect to target token* **then**

13 | information = details + information;

14   **end**

15 **end**

16 **if** *k* **then**

17   **if** *information not in keywords sets* **then**

18 | Append information to information array;

19   **end**

20 **end**

21 **for** *dep* ∈ *words' dependencies* **do**

22   **if** *dep = case and connect to TargetIndex and related to prepositions of or for or from* **then**

23   PrepDetails = result of input TargetIndex to Algorithm 3;

24   LastElement = Take out the last element from information array;

25   information = combine LastElement and PrepDetails;

26   Append information to information array;

27   Send TargetIndex back to Algorithm 2 to find possible target words;

28   **end**

29 **end**

Finally, for basic extraction, a difficult situation that we must handle is the lack of direct dependency between extraction targets. A real case for this situation is presented in Fig. 6, where there is no directly usable (conjunction) dependency between the anchored target (i.e., *name*) and the other target in the sentence (*receipt*). In this case, the only connection between them is indirect through an intermediate noun *theatre*, which is a descriptive detail of *Name* and can be retrieved using Algorithm 4. Thus, we solve this problem by employing this intermediate and returning the words that are the details of the original target (in this case, *theatre*) to Algorithm 2 to obtain our required information (*receipt*). Afterwards, the acquired information is delivered to Algorithm 3 and Algorithm 4 to retrieve their entire information. This recursive process will be terminated when there is no word that must be processed. With this solution, complete information can be obtained (for our example, *theatre_name_for_city* and *receipt_for_booking_performance*), although there is no direct dependency between two targets.

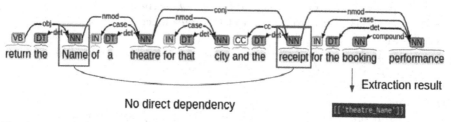

Fig. 6. An example of the lack of a direct dependency between two extraction targets (i.e., *name* and *receipt*).

Advanced Extraction Rules

After the previously introduced approach (basic extraction) has been realized, the implemented system is tested (the experimentation is reported in detail in the next section), and the proposed approach remains insufficient in extracting all intended information from the received natural language-based descriptions. Among all issues, two major insufficiencies are the lack of further details and incorrect extraction outcomes caused by vague NLP annotation results.

Fig. 7. Results of applying the basic and advanced extractions on the same description.

The lack of further details implies that the current approach cannot obtain the complete information required (missing essential segments), which results in unclear and ambiguous processing outcomes. For example, in Fig. 7, in the basic extraction result, the elements behind prepositions *in* and *to* are neglected. Because such unspecific or incomplete outcomes may not be useful or can hamper subsequent applications (e.g., automated service composition or recovery), the current retrieval and extraction must be further improved and enhanced to acquire the whole required information.

Meanwhile, it is confirmed that under certain conditions, some keywords defined for the output tuple can cause incorrect PoS annotations and identification of a vague

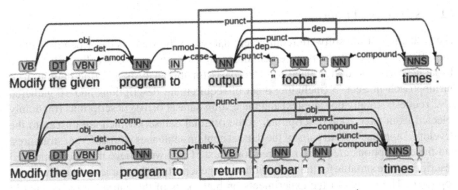

Fig. 8. Dependency parse result after replacing keywords.

NLP dependency (*dep*) between an anchor (keyword) and its first target, which makes the first target not retrieved by using Algorithm 1, as shown at the top of Fig. 8. According to its definition, the *dep* dependency is labeled when an NLP processor cannot determine a more specific relationship for two correlated words. Since it is unspecific, such dependency will hamper following NLP-based applications, including ours (in the demonstrated example, the object dependency between *output* and *times* cannot be identified for Algorithm 1 to work properly).

To address these problems, after the identification and confirmation of the causes of these issues, we design and implement corresponding solutions as additional rules to the previously developed approach (basic extraction) to perform advanced extraction for better tuple-based service demands. First, we revise and enhance Algorithm 3 and Algorithm 4 to enable them to retrieve the descriptive details expressed through the prepositions (including *in*, *to*, and *with*). In addition, the rules to extract different modifiers are added into the approach. An example and result of this enhancement and rule expansion for the first issue are shown in the advanced extraction outcome of Fig. 7 (compared with its basic extraction, a more complete and specific tuple element is obtained, which is clearer and easier to understand). The second issue originates from the adopted NLP tool (i.e., CoreNLP) and the identification and remedy of its root cause within the tool is out of the scope of this study. Hence, a simple but useful method is devised to work around this issue: we automatically replace the keywords that cause this problem with their corresponding stable synonyms, so that a recognizable, concrete dependency identification can be obtained. An example of employing this method is shown at the bottom of Fig. 8, where the required dependency (*obj*) between the keyword (i.e., *output/return*) and its first target (*times*) can be correctly identified.

4 Performance Evaluation

This section presents our experimentation. We first briefly explain the data used for our experiments and subsequently explain the adopted evaluation criteria. Then, the numerical experimental results are reported, analyzed and discussed in the third part of this section.

4.1 Experimental Data

The collection of the software requirement dataset in the study is described in Sect. 2. For different purposes, the requirement descriptions of the dataset are divided into two disparate parts: the design dataset as the basis for the analysis and rule definition of our approach in Sect. 3 (including a set of requirement descriptions and 10 gathered ASC requests, totally 66 samples) and the testing dataset of 108 descriptions (randomly selected from over 1000 descriptions in the original dataset), which are unseen to the developed approach. Both parts of the dataset contain sentences with different structures, and the descriptions are similar to free-form text. Thus, we believe that the comprised descriptions are suitable for the evaluation of the generality and accuracy of the developed approach. The results of the experiments on both parts of the dataset are presented in Sect. 4.3.

4.2 Evaluation Criteria

This section defines the evaluation criteria in this study. First, we introduce four possible categories (i.e., confusion/error matrix) for our extraction results, i.e., true positive (TP), false positive (FP), true negative (TN) and false negative (FN). Afterwards, based on these four categories, four common measures (performance indicators) are defined and used for the assessment and expression of our experimental results: precision, recall, accuracy, and F1 score.

Given a human-written, natural language-based software description, the goal of this study and the proposed approach is to automatically and correctly retrieve its corresponding tuple-based service requirement. Thus, with the manually annotated ground truth data (i.e., the correct answers, as explained in Sect. 2) and the extraction results of the approach, we first consider and calculate the following cases.

True Positive. In this case, for a description or sentence, the tuple elements extracted by the approach match the manually annotated tuple elements of the description (i.e., the correct answers). It is possible that some additional information or repetitive elements are also retrieved by our approach. In such situations, if this additional information or repetitive elements do not affect the judgment of our extraction results, we still classify them into this category.

False Positive. This is also called Type-1 Error. In this case, for a description, the approach retrieves the tuple elements that are not contained in its corresponding ground truth annotation, and they affect its correct judgment. In addition, this category includes the situation in which the system retrieves correct elements with redundant segments that affect their correct judgment.

True Negative. In this case, nothing should be retrieved from a description, and the approach correctly extracts nothing.

False Negative. This is also called Type-2 Error. If the approach misses the intended tuple elements that must be extracted from a description, they will be classified into this category. Moreover, this category includes the situation in which the approach extracts correct elements with insufficient details that make the retrieved tuple elements ambiguous or unclear.

Based on the four categories of extraction results, we define four adopted performance metrics as follows. First, the calculation of accuracy is $(TP + TN)/(TP + TN + FP + FN)$, which is the ratio of correctly predicted cases to the total examined cases. Precision, which is the proportion of correctly predicted positive cases to the total predicted positive cases, is obtained by computing $(TP)/(TP + FP)$. Recall is calculated as $(TP)/(TP + FN)$, which is the ratio of correctly predicted positive cases to all actual cases. Finally, the F1 score is computed as $(2 * Recall * Precision)/(Recall + Precision)$, which is the weighted average of recall and precision and usually applied when FP and FN are not even (different). Larger values of these metrics indicate better performance.

4.3 Performance

With a discussion, this section presents our experimental results. Evaluated by the four adopted metrics, the numerical performance of our basic extraction on the collected dataset is shown in Table 1. First, an overall observation in Table 1 is that the basic extraction approach has high precision performance but relatively poor accuracy and recall results. Based on our manual analysis of the extraction results, the root cause of this phenomenon is the poor FN values (the calculation of both accuracy and recall involves FN), where either the basic extraction cannot retrieve the intended tuple elements from its processed descriptions or the extraction results lack sufficient details (i.e., these two situations are defined for FN in Sect. 4.2) because the defined rules remain incomprehensive and insufficient. Meanwhile, the precision is excellent mainly because the extraction rarely retrieves unwanted tuple elements (i.e., good FP results), since in the dataset, most of the required information (i.e., targets) comes after the anchored keywords, which matches the underlying rationale and basic principle of our extraction approach/pattern. Thus, nothing is usually wrongly retrieved.

Table 1. Experimental results of basic extraction.

Tuple	Dataset	Accuracy	Precision	Recall	F1 score
Input	Design	0.52	0.94	0.52	0.67
Input	Testing	0.60	0.90	0.48	0.63
Output	Design	0.50	0.97	0.51	0.67
Output	Testing	0.65	0.94	0.45	0.61

As mentioned in Sect. 3.3, to improve the results of basic extraction and overcome its insufficiencies, more sophisticated rules to retrieve details are enacted. The resulting approach is called advanced extraction, whose experimental results on the same dataset are demonstrated in Table 2. First, compared with Table 1, a significant improvement in extraction performance is easily observed from Table 2, which proves the effectiveness

Table 2. Experimental results of advanced extraction.

Tuple	Dataset	Accuracy	Precision	Recall	F1 score
Input	Design	0.92	1.00	0.92	0.96
Input	Testing	0.81	0.91	0.81	0.86
Output	Design	0.83	1.00	0.83	0.91
Output	Testing	0.71	0.90	0.58	0.71

of the newly added detailed rules. Second, in Table 2, the performance on the testing dataset remains worse than that on the design dataset because the approach is developed based on the design dataset, and prediction/processing performance is commonly inferior on unseen data (an exception is on the accuracy reported in Table 1). Another main observation is that even on viewable design data, due to the natural constraints of rule-based solutions, it is very difficult to achieve perfect extraction. To achieve better performance, a possible solution is to devise and add more specific rules for different descriptive structures and writing patterns. However, when more rules are defined and their complexity increases, the addition and revision of rules will be more difficult because they can contradict or influence each other, causing unanticipated consequences.

5   Conclusion

In this paper, we first identify that current automated service composition approaches mostly consider and accept only tuple-based service demands. However, for ordinary software stakeholders, the most natural and convenient method to express the requirements is to present them in natural language, which hampers the usability of existing ASC approaches and decreases their degree of automation. Thus, the goal of this study is to automate this transformation process to replace the originally required manual effort, so that it is possible to have a fully automated composition by combining our approach with an existing ASC solution. Thus, based on NLP technology, we proposed and implemented a rule-based extraction approach to precisely parse natural language descriptions and automatically form tuple-based service demands. The extraction rules that are developed and used in our system rely on linguistic information, i.e., the part-of-speech of words and their dependencies, which are offered by a reliable NLP processor and result from manually analyzing and parsing the structures of diverse real requirement sentences to obtain the implied IO elements within the text. Finally, the performance evaluation of the defined rules and preprocessing methods run on a self-collective, real-world software requirement dataset, which is another major contribution of this study. To the best of our knowledge, it is the first dataset for such a research topic, and it can be used by others for further research. Overall, the experimental results demonstrate an acceptable performance, but further improvement is required to gain higher applicability and reliability. In our experiments, the relationship between the acquired system performance and the complexity of the adopted rules and its possible causes have been shown and discussed in detail. In addition, we have identified the main issues that restrict and hamper the performance of rule-based solutions.

Based on this study, it is feasible to use NLP technology and rule-based mechanisms to address the identified and targeted research problem. However, the main difficulty of this research problem lies in the diversity in the structures and types of human sentences: for each specific sentence type or structure, a dedicated NLP rule or preprocessing method must be defined. Thus, the development of a general solution is costly and time-consuming, and it is inefficient to develop it by manually parsing sentences and defining rules for them. To address this difficulty, as a future research direction, we plan to employ learning-based machine learning techniques to automatically determine the required rules or models for our extraction tasks.

Acknowledgments. This research is partially sponsored by the Ministry of Science and Technology (Taiwan) under Grant MOST 108-2221-E-001-007-MY2.

References

1. Li, Z., O'Brien, L.: Towards effort estimation for web service compositions using classification matrix. Int. J. Adv. Internet Technol. **3**, 245–260 (2010)
2. Fanjiang, Y.-Y., Syu, Y., Ma, S.-P., Kuo, J.-Y.: An overview and classification of service description approaches in automated service composition research. IEEE Trans. Serv. Comput. **10**(2), 176–189 (2017)
3. Pop, F.-C., Cremene, M., Vaida, M., Riveill, M.: Natural language service composition with request disambiguation. In: Maglio, P.P., Weske, M., Yang, J., Fantinato, M. (eds.) ICSOC 2010. LNCS, vol. 6470, pp. 670–677. Springer, Heidelberg (2010). https://doi.org/10.1007/978-3-642-17358-5_54
4. Pop, F.C., Cremene, M., Vaida, M.F., Riveill, M.: On-demand service composition based on natural language requests. In: 2009 Sixth International Conference on Wireless On-Demand Network Systems and Services, 2–4 February 2009, pp. 45-48 (2009). https://doi.org/10.1109/WONS.2009.4801832
5. Pop, F.-C., Cremene, M., Tigli, J.-Y., Lavirotte, S., Riveill, M., Vaida, M.: Natural language based on-demand service composition. Int. J. Comput. Commun. Control 871–883 (2010). https://hal.archives-ouvertes.fr/hal-00564613 (in English)
6. Cremene, M., Tigli, J.Y., Lavirotte, S., Pop, F.C., Riveill, M., Rey, G.: Service composition based on natural language requests. In: 2009 IEEE International Conference on Services Computing, 21–25 September 2009, pp. 486–489 (2009). https://doi.org/10.1109/SCC.2009.43
7. Manning, C.D., Surdeanu, M., Bauer, J., Finkel, J.R., Bethard, S., McClosky, D.: The Stanford CoreNLP natural language processing toolkit. In: Proceedings of 52nd Annual Meeting of the Association for Computational Linguistics: System Demonstrations, pp. 55–60 (2014)
8. Zhang, N., Wang, J., Ma, Y.: Mining domain knowledge on service goals from textual service descriptions. IEEE Trans. Serv. Comput. **13**(3), 488–502 (2017)
9. https://leetcode.com/. Accessed
10. De Marneffe, M.-C., Manning, C.D.: Stanford typed dependencies manual. Technical report, Stanford University (2008)

Forecast of Electric Vehicle Charging Load in Urban Planning – A Study in Shenzhen

Yiguan Ma[1] and Xing Wang[2(✉)]

[1] Shenzhen Polytechnic, Shenzhen 518055, Guangdong, People's Republic of China
[2] Shenzhen Urban Planning and Land Resources Research Center, Shenzhen 518034, People's Republic of China

Abstract. With the rapid expansion of volume of electric vehicles in China's transportation system, forecast of the electricity charging load poses challenges in urban planning and grid planning. This article, based on the rudimentary daily operation data of electric vehicles in Shenzhen, made short-term and long-term forecast of charging load. Forecast of the charging load mainly refers to volume of electric vehicles, daily power demand, charging load distribution. Considering the differences in driving characters and vehicle usages, totally 6 categories of vehicles were analyzed in this article. Findings in this article will provide important information for charging pile planning and power grid planning, and put forward constructive opinions for urban services and management.

Keywords: Electric vehicle · Charging load forecast · Charging pile planning

1 Introduction

For achieving the goals of "carbon emission neutrality" and "carbon emission peak", the past ten years witnessed the rapid expansion of electric vehicles (EVs) volume entering Chinese transportation system, especially in large Chinese cities. However, until currently, attention on the field of forecasting the charging load of EVs is inadequate. That is, the concentration of charging load may put tremendous pressure on the surrounding power grids, and the rapid development of EVs, with highly concentrated charging load of electric network in urban system, poses new challenges for urban planning.

Take Shenzhen as a typical example. Being one of the 13 pilot cities for the demonstration and promotion of EVs in China, Shenzhen has been demonstrating and promoting new energy vehicles in the three major areas of public transportation, official business and family vehicles for more than ten years. As of June 2019, Shenzhen has promoted a total of 270,000 electric vehicles of various types, of which electric buses, electric taxis, electric logistics vehicles and electric private cars are the main ones. However, the latest version of Shenzhen's special electric power plan does not take into account of the development trend of charging loads. Future electric power special plans or detailed

© Springer Nature Switzerland AG 2022
A. Katangur and L.-J. Zhang (Eds.): SCC 2021, LNCS 12995, pp. 18–32, 2022.
https://doi.org/10.1007/978-3-030-96566-2_2

municipal plans are necessary to be further improved, and there are still deficiencies in the forecast of electric vehicle load power consumption.

This article conducted charging load forecast for providing basic data in planning of charging piles and relevant urban services, based on the electricity consumption of different types of EVs in Shenzhen. Major factors that were considered as affecting the charging load of electric vehicles include electric vehicle scale, initial state of charge, charging power, charging time, and battery capacity.

2 Methodology

2.1 Forecast of Charging Load of EVs

2.1.1 Factors Affecting Charging Load of EVs

The charging load of electric vehicles is determined by the average daily electricity demand and the distribution of charging time. The main factors that need to be considered in urban power grid planning include the scale of electric vehicles, charging power, charging time, and power battery capacity. In the process of calculating electricity load forecasting, electricity consumption habits and electricity price factors are also important reference indicators.

The usage habits of various electric vehicles are the most important factor that affects the changing trend of electric vehicle charging loads. For example, electric buses run on roads most of the time every day, so charging will be concentrated outside the lunch break and night operating hours; taxis are charged during the daytime during lunch breaks when there is less business; the driving time of private cars is mainly concentrated in the peak period of commuting, the charging behavior mainly occurs during the night break. In addition, the similar use habits of similar cars are the regular part of the disorderly charging behavior of electric vehicles, which is the basis for the analysis of electric vehicle load characteristics.

2.1.2 Typical Charging Load Characteristic Curve

A typical charging load characteristic curve expresses the distribution of daily electricity consumption in various periods, showing fluctuations caused by the inconsistent charging habits of electric vehicle drivers. Therefore, the charging habits determine the changing trend of the daily charging load characteristics of electric vehicles.

The maximum load and its appearance time are the main concerns of the charging load characteristic curve. Since the size of the charging load of the power system changes with time, there will inevitably be a maximum value within a certain time interval, which is called the maximum load. The maximum load that occurs between 0 and 24 h is called the daily maximum load, and the maximum load that occurs throughout the year is called the annual maximum load. The maximum load is usually the target value of load forecasting, usually expressed as P_{max}, and the unit is kilowatt, ten thousand kilowatt or megawatt. The occurrence time of the maximum load directly affects the control decision of the grid dispatching on the grid. There will also be a minimum value of electricity load every day, called the minimum load, which is represented by P_{min}. Similarly, according to the load data of each sampling point, the average load of the day can be obtained, which is represented by P_{av}, and P_{av} can also be obtained by dividing the total daily electricity consumption by 24.

According to P_{max}, P_{av} and P_{min}, the maximum load rate α and minimum load rate β of the electrical load can be obtained, where $\alpha = P_{max}/P_{av}$ and $\beta = P_{min}/P_{av}$. These two data represent the distribution of the applied electric load curve. The stronger the curve fluctuation, the larger the value of α and the smaller the value of β. The more stable the curve is, the opposite is true.

2.2 The Current Situation of EVs in Shenzhen

Shenzhen's electric vehicles could be divided into six categories, including electric buses, electric taxis, electric logistics vehicles, electric private cars, electric ride-hailing vehicles, and electric dump trucks. At the current stage, the electric buses and electric taxis are occupying 100% of the market, and the electric vehicles are expected to dominate the logistics transportation system in the near future. However, the construction of charging facilities in Shenzhen cannot match the development speed of electric vehicles, leading to problems such as stray charging of electric buses (some bus parking lots do not have the conditions to build charging piles), and electric taxis queuing up for charging (Table 1).

Table 1. Volume of electric vehicles in Shenzhen (until June, 2019)

Category	Volume
Electric buses	16359
Electric taxis	21485
Electric logistics vehicles	61587
Electric private cars	142000
Electric ride-hailing vehicles	21912
Electric dump trucks	5104
Total	268447

Data source: the authors.

The charging load characteristics of electric vehicle charging facilities are the superposition of the load characteristics of all electric vehicle charging facilities in Shenzhen. Considering the differences of EVs' characters, such as categories, drivers' using habits, and the development levels of charging facilities, the article will make forecast of charging load of each of the types.

3 The Charging Load Forecast

3.1 Daily Electricity Demand Calculation

3.1.1 The Average Daily Electricity Demand of Each Unit

The average daily electricity demand of electric vehicles is reflected in the average daily fuel consumption of petrol vehicles, which is determined by the average daily mileage and average energy consumption of vehicles:

Average daily electricity demand = power consumption per kilometer * average daily mileage

Based on this function, the daily electricity demand of each unit of each category of EVs in Shenzhen was calculated as followed.

(1) *The average daily electricity demand of electric buses*
The driving route of electric buses is determined by the operating company. According to the statistics of the three major bus companies, the average daily mileage of buses in Shenzhen is about 190 km. However, due to insufficient bus parking stations in Shenzhen and uneven distribution of charging facilities, many electric buses need to be recharged remotely, so the average daily mileage is 200 km. Through statistical comprehensive calculations, Shenzhen's electric buses can support 0.88 km of electric buses per kilowatt-hour of electricity, that is, their average energy consumption per 100 km is 113 kWh. Therefore, based on the above two points, the daily electricity demand of Shenzhen buses is about 226 kWh.

(2) *The average daily electricity demand of electric taxis*
The driving route of electric taxis is not fixed. According to the "Shenzhen New Energy Vehicle Charging Facilities Layout Plan", the average daily mileage of electric taxis in Shenzhen is about 350 km. The driving time is distributed at noon and a few hours before the driver-shift. The model of Shenzhen electric taxi is BYD E6, which has 5 seats, weighs about 2.2T, and consumes about 20 kWh per hundred kilometers. According to preliminary calculations, the average daily electricity demand for electric taxis in Shenzhen is about 70 kWh.

(3) *The average daily electricity demand of logistics vehicle*
Shenzhen logistics vehicles can be categorized as light trucks and minivans. Light trucks weigh about 3T and carry 1.2T (Dongfeng EV350). The power consumption per 100 km is about 35 kWh. The main charging time is at night; The weight of the micro-face car is about 1.6T, the load capacity is 800 kg (BYD T3), the power consumption is about 20 kWh per hundred kilometers, and the main charging time is at night. After the weighted calculation of the two types of vehicles, the power consumption per 100 km of Shenzhen's electric logistics vehicles should be 25 kWh. According to the average daily mileage of logistics vehicles in Shenzhen is about 80 km, the average daily electricity demand should be 20 kWh.

(4) *The average daily electricity demand of private cars*
The driving habits of private cars in Shenzhen are various according to the needs of car drivers. According to the survey results of private car travel in Shenzhen, the average daily mileage of electric private cars in Shenzhen is about 30 km. Although

there are various types of private cars in Shenzhen, weight of them is between 1.3T–2.0T, and the power consumption per 100 km is about 15–20 kWh. Taking into account the air-conditioning power consumption and battery consumption of electric private cars in summer, the electric power consumption per 100 km of electric private cars is calculated at 20 kWh, and the average daily power demand is about 6 kWh.

(5) *The average daily electricity demand of online car-hailing*

According to the "Shenzhen City's New Energy Vehicle Charging Facilities Layout Plan", the average daily mileage of online car-hailing in Shenzhen is about 200 km. Electric car-hailing mainly uses BYD Qin and Dongfeng EV250 models, with energy consumption per 100 km In the range of 15–20 kWh. The travel rate of online car-hailing is calculated at 50%, and the average daily power consumption of each online car is about 20 kWh.

(6) *The average daily electricity demand of dump truck*

According to the introduction of electric dump trucks in Sect. 4.1.2, the main model of Shenzhen electric dump trucks is BYDT10YT. The BYDT10YT electric dump truck weighs more than 10 tons, weighs close to 20 tons under full load, has a battery capacity of 435 kWh, a cruising range of 280 km, and an energy consumption of about 150 kWh per hundred kilometers. According to the survey results, the average daily mileage of electric dump trucks is about 200 km, and the average daily electricity demand is about 300 kWh (Table 2).

Table 2. Daily electricity demand of each unit

Category	Weight (Ton)	Energy consumption per hundred kilometers (kw.h)	Average daily mileage (km)	Electricity demand (kw.h)
Electric buses	>=12	113	200	226
Electric taxis	2.2	20	350	70
Electric logistics vehicles	2–4	25	80	20
Electric private cars	1.3–2	20	30	6
Electric ride-hailing vehicles	1.5	20	50	10
Electric dump trucks	>=0	150	100	150

Data source: the authors.

3.1.2   Forecast of Daily Electricity Demand in Shenzhen

According to the forecast of the number of various types of electric vehicles, combined with the analysis of the average daily power consumption demand of various types of electric vehicles in this section, the total power demand of various types of electric vehicles can be obtained. At the same time, according to summer electric vehicles will use an additional 10% of electric energy as air conditioning load, the total electricity demand of various electric vehicles in summer can be further obtained (Table 3).

Table 3. Forecast of daily electricity demand of EVs in Shenzhen

Category	Average demand per unit	Near-future			Long-term		
		Volume	Average demand (million kWh)	Summer average demand (million kWh)	Volume	Average demand (million kWh)	Summer average demand (million kWh)
Electric buses	226	16,359	3.7	4.07	20,000	4.52	5
Electric taxis	70	22,000	1.54	1.7	25,000	1.75	1.93
Electric logistics vehicles	20	80,000	1.6	1.76	150,000	3	3.3
Electric private cars	6	200,000	1.2	1.32	2,000,000	12	13.2
Electric ride-hailing vehicles	10	25,000	0.5	0.55	70,000	1.4	1.56
Electric dump trucks	150	4,000	1.2	1.32	4,000	1.20	1.32
total		347,359	9.74	10.66	2,269,000	23.87	26.26

3.2   Distribution of Daily Charging Load of EVs of Different Category

This section carries out calculation of the distribution of electric charging load analysis via characteristic load curve. Various categories of electric vehicles will be discussed separately.

3.2.1   Distribution of Charging Load of Public Buses

In terms of usage habits, the operating hours of Shenzhen electric buses are between 6:00 am and 9:00 pm, so the charging load during this period is relatively low. Due to the long driving range and short battery life of some electric buses, it is necessary to make up for a short period of time between 12:00–14:00 noon to form a small peak in the charging load of electric buses during the day. Electricity prices have a decisive influence on the load characteristics of electric buses. The valley electricity price is much lower than the peak and flat electricity prices. Therefore, in order to save costs, Shenzhen electric buses tend to charge during the electricity price valley. Since 23:00 is the junction of the electricity price valley period and the peace period, electric bus operators usually choose to start charging at 23:00, resulting in the charging load concentrated around 23:00. However, since it is impossible for electric buses to start charging after the battery is completely exhausted, Shenzhen bus companies require that the battery of electric buses need to retain at least 20% of the power. Different bus routes have different mileage and battery usage. Different, therefore, it is difficult for major operating units to guarantee stable charging during the electricity price valley period, and more than 20% of the charging capacity will be charged during the electricity price peak or normal period.

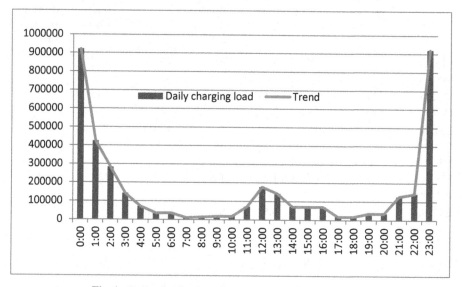

Fig. 1. Daily distribution of charging load of electric buses

As shown in Fig. 1, 50% of the daily charging capacity of electric buses will be concentrated between 23:00 and 1:00. It can be seen from Fig. 1 that the maximum load of electric buses appears at 23:00, the maximum load value during the day appears at 12:00 noon, and the minimum load appears at 7:00. The maximum load factor α is 624%, and the minimum load factor β is 7.2%.

3.2.2 Distribution of Charging Load of Electric Taxis

The main model of Shenzhen electric taxi is BYD E6, which is charged by social public charging stations. At this stage, the number of public charging piles in Shenzhen is relatively small and the layout is relatively concentrated, resulting in a relatively concentrated charging behavior of electric taxis. At some charging stations, electric taxis often line up for charging during lunch break charging peaks. This is mainly because the replacement speed of electric vehicles in Shenzhen is higher than the speed of the construction of charging facilities. This situation should be temporary. As of 2020, Shenzhen is expected to build more than 10,000 fast-charging piles with a vehicle-to- pile ratio of approximately 2:1. In this case, the charging behavior of Shenzhen electric taxis will be more scattered, and the charging load characteristic curve will be more even.

The operating hours of electric taxis in Shenzhen are unlimited, that is, 24 h a day. In this way, there is no situation where similar electric bus charging behavior occurs outside of operating hours. BYD's e6 electric taxi has a cruising range of 300 km, a battery capacity of 60 kWh, and a daily mileage of about 350 km. Considering that electric taxi drivers need to reserve 20% of the electricity for emergency use, it is preliminary estimated that Shenzhen's electric taxis will need it every day Charge 2–3 times. Noon 12:00–14:00 is the free time for taxi operation, this time is the peak time for electric taxi charging during the day.

Since electric taxi charging mainly uses charging piles in social charging stations and charging piles in social public parking lots. The electricity used in these two places belongs to industrial and commercial electricity. Therefore, the charging of electric taxis will also be affected by peaks and valleys. Due to the impact of electricity prices, charging behavior will also be concentrated at night. Since 23:00 is the demarcation point of Shenzhen's peak and valley electricity prices, there will be a peak period of charging load 1–2 h after 23:00.

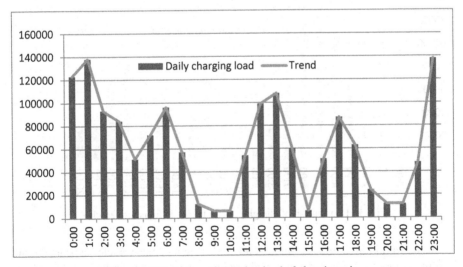

Fig. 2. Distribution of charging load of electric taxis

As shown in Fig. 2, the maximum load of electric taxis appears around 12:00, and the minimum load appears at 9:00. The maximum load factor α is 278%, and the minimum load factor β is 9.6%.

3.2.3 Distribution of Charging Load of Electric Logistics Vehicles

The usage habits of electric logistics vehicles in Shenzhen vary greatly on the business they carry out. The traveling modes could be divided into two types: daytime and night-time. Since the electric logistics vehicles operating express delivery business mainly travel during the day, the charging time is mainly at night, and the electricity price is mainly selected for charging; electric logistics vehicles operating in the distribution business of agricultural and sideline products such as fruits and vegetables are used to purchase goods in the evening to the first half of the night. For delivery in the early morning, the charging time is customarily scheduled in the afternoon; the operation time of electric logistics vehicles that deliver goods to major shopping malls is mainly concentrated in the first half of the night or morning, and the charging time will be scheduled in the second half of the night and noon.

Electric logistics vehicles have various operating methods, but their relative operating methods and quantity structure are relatively stable. Generally speaking, electric logistics vehicles are similar to electric taxis and buses. The charging behavior rarely occurs in the morning. During the lunch break, the business idle period is also the peak period of charging load. At the same time, because electric logistics vehicles mainly use industrial electricity or Commercial electricity consumption will also be affected by peak and valley electricity prices, and there will be a peak charging period after 23:00.

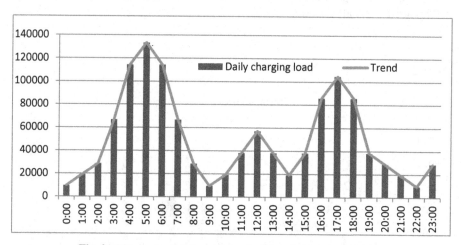

Fig. 3. Distribution of charging load of electric logistics vehicles

As shown in Fig. 3, the maximum load of electric logistics vehicles appears around 5:00 in the morning, the maximum load in the daytime appears around 17:00, and the minimum load appears around 9:00. The maximum load factor α is about 267%, and the minimum load factor β is about 19%.

3.2.4 Distribution of Charging Load of Electric Private Cars

Shenzhen's electric private cars mainly include BYD Song/Han/Tang, Dongfeng EV350, etc., which are generally charged by self-use charging piles. According to the "Shenzhen

New Energy Vehicle Charging Facilities Layout Plan" (in compilation), the average daily mileage of private cars in Shenzhen does not exceed 30 km, and the daily charging demand is about 6 kWh. If a 7-kW slow charging pile is used, only it takes 1 h to be fully charged. If the private car owner has a fixed parking space, and the parking space has the conditions to build a charging pile, then, for the vast majority of private car owners, they only need to charge once a day at night. It can be seen that private car charging will be concentrated at night. According to the above, the average charging time of a private car is usually about three hours. Assuming that the start time of a private car power outage is the time when the owner returns to the residential area (20:00–23:00), the charging time at night will mainly focus on 20:00–24:00. However, electric private cars may also need temporary power supplements. Some car owners may not have parking spaces that meet the conditions for building charging piles. Therefore, many electric private car owners need to supplement power during the day.

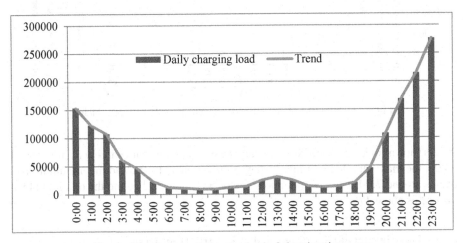

Fig. 4. Distribution of charging load of electric private cars

As shown in Fig. 4, the maximum load of electric private car charging occurs around 23:00, the maximum load during the day occurs around 13:00, and the minimum load occurs around 7:00. The maximum load factor α is about 312%, and the minimum load factor β is about 17%.

3.2.5 Distribution of Charging Load of Ride-hailing Vehicles

The automobile online booking industry is an emerging industry that has gradually grown into scale in Shenzhen in recent years, and it is also an industry that has gradually grown with the development of new energy vehicles as an opportunity. The models used in the Shenzhen online car industry are mainly BYD Qin EV series or Dongfeng EV series electric cars.

The usage and charging habits of electric car-hailing are relatively close to those of private cars, and the electricity demand is low. The daily electricity demand is about 10 kWh. If a 40-kW fast charging pile is used for charging, it only takes 15 min to fully charge.

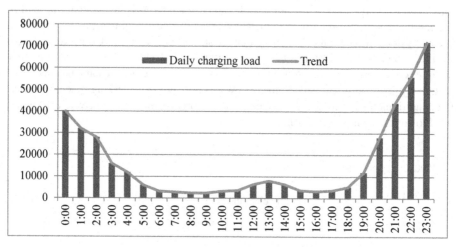

Fig. 5. Distribution of charging load of electric ride-hailing vehicles

As shown in Fig. 5, the maximum load of electric private car charging occurs around 23:00, the maximum load during the day occurs around 13:00, and the minimum load occurs around 7:00. The maximum load factor α is about 312%, and the minimum load factor β is about 17%.

3.2.6 Distribution of Charging Load of Electric Dump Trucks

Electric dump truck is a type of electric vehicle that has only recently begun to be promoted. It is estimated that the current scale is about 500 vehicles, and the short-term and long-term scale is 4000 vehicles. Although the number of electric dump trucks accounts for a small proportion of the total amount of electric vehicles, because the electric dump truck weighs close to 20T when fully loaded, and the average daily mileage exceeds 100 km, the demand for electricity is huge. The charging of dump trucks mainly adopts mobile charging stations arranged at work or parking sites. Since the transportation time of electric dump trucks is mainly concentrated at night, the charging mode of electric dump trucks is more flexible, and the charging load will be mainly concentrated in the daytime. Since the charging of electric dump trucks will not be affected by the charging facilities, it is expected that the distribution of the charging load of electric dump trucks will be more evenly distributed during the day.

As shown in Fig. 6, the maximum load of the electric dump truck charging load appears around 12:00 noon, and the minimum load appears around 0:00 at night. The maximum load factor α is about 197%, and the minimum load factor β is about 17%.

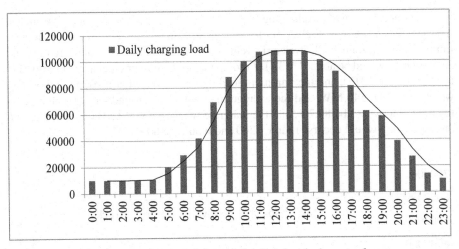

Fig. 6. Distribution of charging load of electric dump truck

3.3 Short-Term and Long-Term Forecasts of Electric Vehicle Charging Load in Shenzhen

This article used the trend extrapolation method to do the short-term and long-term forecasts of charging load of different categories of EVs in Shenzhen. The maximum and minimum loads of various electric vehicles in different periods and their appearance times can be found in Table 4.

Table 4. Forecast of charging load of different categories of EVs in Shenzhen

		Buses	Taxis	Logistics	Private cars	Ride-hailing	Dump truck
Short-term	Maximum load	960 MW	200 MW	196 MW	172 MW	83 MW	108 MW
	Appearance time	23:00	12:00	5:00	23:00	23:00	12:00
	Minimum load	11 MW	6.1 MW	10.5 MW	8 MW	3.3 MW	9.2 MW
	Appearance time	7:00	10:00	9:00	8:00	8:00	1:00
Long-term	Maximum load	1175 MW	224 MW	367 MW	1720 MW	234 MW	108 MW
	Appearance time	23:00	12:00	5:00	23:00	23:00	12:00
	Minimum load	18 MW	7.7 MW	26 MW	80 MW	9.4 MW	9.2 MW
	Appearance time	7:00	10:00	9:00	8:00	8:00	1:00

With combination of the charging load of the above 6 categories of electric vehicles, we can achieve the overall charging load of EVs in Shenzhen (Fig. 7). As in the near future, the maximum load of electric vehicles in Shenzhen will be appeared around 23:00, which would be about 1353 MW (compared to the maximum load of 17,500 MW in Shenzhen in 2017), and the minimum load will be appeared at 9:00 in the morning, which would be 140 MW, and the average load would be around 445 MW, the peak-to-valley rate would be 89.7%, and the load rate would be 32.9%. The maximum load during the day would occurs around 12:00 and would be 603 MW.

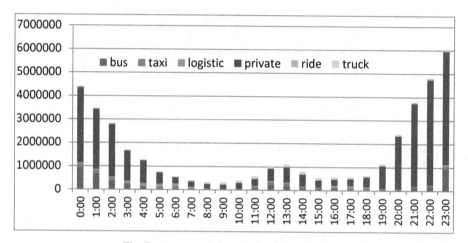

Fig. 7. Forecast of charging load in near future

The maximum load of the long-term charging of electric vehicles in Shenzhen occurs at 23:00, which is approximately 3,300 MW. The maximum load during the day occurs at 13:00 at noon, which is approximately 950 MW, and the minimum load occurs at 9:00, which is approximately 240. MW, the average load is about 1100 MW, the peak-to-valley rate is 92.7%, and the load rate is 33.3%. At the maximum load, the charging load of electric buses, taxis, logistics vehicles, private cars, online car-hailing and dump trucks accounted for 35.5%, 3.0%, 2.4%, 51.8%, 7%, and 0.3%, respectively (Fig. 8).

In the long-term planning period, as special vehicles such as public transportation, logistics, and taxis in Shenzhen have become saturated, there will be no significant increase in electricity demand. At the same time, as fuel vehicles continue to reach their service life, the number of electric private vehicles. The number of electric vehicles will continue to rise, which will be much higher than the number of other types of electric vehicles, and the demand for electricity will gradually exceed that of other types of electric vehicles. Therefore, in the composition of the overall electric vehicle charging load, the proportion of electric private vehicle charging load will continue to increase. The charging load will be more concentrated at night.

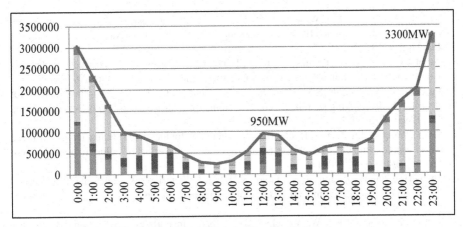

Fig. 8. Forecast of charging load in the long term

4 Conclusion

This article conducted charging load forecast for providing basic data in planning of charging piles and relevant urban services, based on the electricity consumption of different types of EVs in Shenzhen. Major factors that were considered as affecting the charging load of electric vehicles include electric vehicle scale, initial state of charge, charging power, charging time, and battery capacity.

According to the analysis, the electricity demand of electric vehicles is mainly reflected in two aspects, including the electricity consumption and the charging load characteristics. Electricity consumption is mainly related to the average daily mileage and energy conversion efficiency of electric vehicles, and the load characteristics are related to the charging habits of electric vehicle owners or operating units.

With the continuous promotion of electric vehicles in Shenzhen, the demand for electricity consumption of various electric vehicles will also increase proportionally. In terms of load characteristics, the peak electricity load of electric vehicles mainly occurs around 23:00, and the trough of electricity consumption is mainly concentrated at 7:00–9:00 am.

According the findings, in the short-term, the electricity demand of electric buses in Shenzhen will be close to 40% of the total demand, and the charging load of electric buses has a greater impact on the overall charging load of the city. In the long run, as the number of electric private cars will far exceed other types of electric vehicles, the electricity demand of electric private cars will become the most important part of the electricity demand of electric vehicles, directly determining the scale and trend of charging load.

References

1. Yan, C., Zechun, H., Xiaoyu, D.: Overview of research on electric vehicle operation optimization considering the flexibility of charging demand space. Power Syst. Technol. **3**(45), 1–16 (2021)

2. Ping, L., Sheng, C., Yan, W., Qiaoyong, C.: Electric vehicle charging load forecasting considering user travel characteristics. J. Huazhong Univ. Sci. Technol. (Natural Science Edition) **48**(11), 126–132 (2020)
3. Jianhua, O., Chongchao, P., Xuan, Z., Tai, J., Tianqi, L., Yongzhen, W.: Electric vehicle charging load prediction based on charging behavior analysis. Electr. Meas. Instrum. 1–9 (2021)
4. Xu Zhiwei, H., Zechun, S.Y., Hongcai, Z., Xiaoshuang, C.: Orderly charging strategy for electric vehicle charging stations based on dynamic time-of-use electricity prices. Proc. Chin. Soc. Electr. Eng. **34**(22), 3638–3646 (2014)
5. Ma, Y., Wang H., Lu, Z.: Two-level coordinated planning for location and capacity of distributed power sources with electric vehicles taking into account the effect of failure rate. Power Syst. Technol. **3**(45), 1–12 (2021)
6. Zhang Hongcai, H., Zechun, S.Y., Zhiwei, X., Long, J.: Electric vehicle charging load forecasting method considering temporal and spatial distribution. Autom. Electr. Power Syst. **38**(01), 13–20 (2014)
7. Runsen, Z., Zhang Junyi, W., Wenchao, J.Y.: Urban transportation low-carbon development path based on land use-transport-energy integration model: taking Changzhou as an example. Urban Reg. Plann. Res. **12**(02), 57–73 (2020)
8. Yue, Z., et al.: Calculation method of electric vehicle baseline load based on classification. IOP Conf. Ser. Earth Environ. Sci. **791**(1) (2021)
9. Zhiqiang, Z., Xiang, Z., Hua, C., Donghua, C., Yulong, J.: Orderly charging strategy and system implementation of large-scale electric vehicles in residential quarters. Foreign Electr. Meas. Technol. **40**(03), 118–122 (2021)

A Survey: The State-of-the-Art Development of B-Learning Services

Yi Li[1]([✉]), Jinhong Xu[1], and Xinyu Lin[2]

[1] Shenzhen Institute of Information Technology, Shenzhen 518172, Guangdong, People's Republic of China
[2] Shenzhen Polytechnic, Shenzhen 518172, Guangdong, People's Republic of China

Abstract. Blended learning in recent years has received intensive attentions in education, which combines the traditional offline teaching and emerging online teaching to improve the learning effects. For blended learning, there are many hot topics which are required to explore. In this paper, we comprehensively survey the state-of-the-art development of blended learning, specifically, we review the connotation and types of blended learning and further six patterns of blended learning are clearly discussed in detail, they are face-to-face driver, rotation, online lab, flex, self-blend and online driver. The applications of these patterns are fully summarized according to existing works. Also we compare the blended learning with traditional learning and online learning in locations, learning approaches, technology use, flexibility, sense of participation, interaction and evaluation. Finally, to improve the effects of blended learning, we present two strategies for optimizing blended learning, one is using intelligent technologies augment teacher preparations, another is building customized learning experience.

Keywords: Blended learning · Education services · Learning pattern

1 Introduction

With the development of IT and communication technologies, the traditional face-to-face one-way transmission teaching mode can not meet the needs of students. At present, the novel teaching mode has emerged, and this new teaching mode has become a topic of public concern.

Blended Learning (B-Learning) is a kind of learning strategy and learning concept that has gradually gained attention since e-learning got so complicated and traditional classroom learning returned. B-learning has two goals: learning and teaching, and it is guided by multiple learning concepts. It is a teaching strategy that combines face-to-face teaching, e-learning and practical teaching according to the learning content, students' conditions, and teachers' own conditions.

To demonstrate the state-of-the-art development of B-Learning, we survey the main works in related domain and further we conduct the contrastive analysis

© Springer Nature Switzerland AG 2022
A. Katangur and L.-J. Zhang (Eds.): SCC 2021, LNCS 12995, pp. 33–42, 2022.
https://doi.org/10.1007/978-3-030-96566-2_3

of multiple learning mode, the purpose is to propose the optimizing strategies of B-learning in actual application scenarios.

The reminder of this paper is summarized as follows: In Sect. 2, we survey the state-of-the-art development of B-Learning, Sect. 3 introduces the contrastive analysis of multiple learning model, we give the optimizing strategies of B-Learning in Sect. 4. Conclusions are given in Sect. 5.

2   The State-of-the-Art of B-Learning

2.1   The Connotation and Types of B-Learning

Ho Kekang [7] understands blended Learning as combining the advantages of traditional Learning methods with the advantages of e-learning (i.e. digital Learning or e-learning). It means student-oriented and teacher-led, which changes the roles of teachers and students. Teachers can guide, support, supervise and control, and students can make full use of the environment created by teachers to carry out learning freely and autonomously. In the work of [10], Li Jiahou believes that B-Learning is a integrated learning. He focuses on the optimal combination of teaching media, teaching methods and teaching strategies, i.e., optimizing teaching and promoting learning through rational use of teaching practice process. From another perspective, B-Learning can be regarded as the organic integration of face-to-face classroom learning and online learning [11]. Its core concept is to start from the problem to seek ideas and ways to solve the problem. In the teaching process, appropriate teaching media and knowledge transmission methods should be adopted, it can ensure the minimum investment, but the benefit of the maximum harvest.

Jennifer Hofraann [8] described it as follows: Blended learning is supported by a new idea. Instructors or program designers divide it into several stages according to the characteristics of the teaching process, and optimize the teaching of each stage, so as to realize the overall understanding and mastery of learners. Michael Orey [14] believes that blended learning should be defined from the perspectives of learners, teachers or instructional designers and instructional managers. According to his understanding, blended learning should consider the initial ability of learners, the information literacy of teaching scheme designers and the real entity teaching environment. The American association of training and development (ASTD) Singh and Reed [16] also think B-learning is a kind of study way, described as the quantitatively appropriate technology, the combination of good learning personality, time and space will be awarded the fit into the right skills, so as to complete the knowledge and achieve the teaching goal.

Although scholars have different definitions of blended learning, there are not many differences in essence. In a broad sense, blended learning is generally considered to be the combination of traditional teaching and network teaching to achieve the purpose of complementary advantages and reflect the leader-subject role of constructivism. In the narrow sense, it is considered as the optimal combination of teaching methods, media, mode, content, resources, environment and other teaching elements to achieve the purpose of optimizing teaching.

2.2   The Patterns of B-Learning

With the development and definition for connotation of B-Learning, many patterns of B-Learning have been presented in academia, this section will summarize the popular patterns in existing B-Learning [15].

Face-to-Face Driver. In this pattern, teachers can deliver their courses via face-to-face mode. By using the online learning, the teacher use it as a supplement or reinforcement for off-line teaching. In the face to face model, almost all education will take place offline. That means it will be given personally to students the way traditional education has always been. Network elements exist to try and deal with specific problems that some students may have. For example, if a student starts to be disruptive because he or she is bored, the teacher may use online resources to reengage the student.

In this sense, the face-to-face learning model is actually a hybrid learning method used to complement standard teaching techniques. It uses classroom technology, such as classroom tablets, as a teaching resource for individual students, so that other students can make solid progress through face-to-face instruction.

Rotation. Students work in a cycle of independent online learning and face-to-face classroom time. It is a course or subject in which students take turns in different modes of study, at least one of which is online, according to a fixed schedule or at the discretion of the teacher. Other forms may include activities such as group or whole-class mentoring, group projects, individual tutoring, and pencil-and-paper assignments. With the exception of homework, students mostly study on physical campuses.

Online Lab. All courses are conducted via a digital platform, but in a fixed physical location. Students often take traditional courses in this mode as well. In the online lab model, education takes place entirely online, but in a physical classroom. Students still have a physics classroom environment, but it's being transformed into a technology-based environment. There are no required teachers, but instead paralegals who supervise and assist students where possible. It is known to be used by schools around the world with particularly tight budgets. It can also help any student who needs to move at a different pace. Since all courses are delivered online, students can work on the course at their own pace, with no one falling behind or staying put.

Flex. Regarding to this pattern, most of the courses are offered through digital platforms where teachers can provide face-to-face counseling and support. For most teachers, the flexible teaching model may be seem unusual and not common in a traditional classroom setting. The Flex model relies heavily on online instruction, although much of it is taught in physical schools.

In this model, teachers act more as facilitators, providing complementary support rather than specialized guidance. Their roles do include some offline activities, including face-to-face support, group mentoring or personal coaching.

In the elastic model, students can flexibly adjust in a subject at their own pace, independent of the rest of the class. This allows the approach to be tailored to the needs of each student. This is why we often see the resilience model adopted in classes where students are perceived to be at risk.

Self-blend. Students choose to augment their traditional learning through online courses. In self-blended learning, students participate in traditional teaching in the physics classroom in the way we are all used to. Students will supplement their online learning with additional classes or online instruction. It's up to individual students to decide, which is why it's more likely to be done by older, independent and motivated students.

Online Driver. Students complete the entire course through an online platform, possibly with a teacher checking in. All classes and instructions are conducted through a digital platform, with face-to-face meetings scheduled or provided if necessary. Given the rise of modern technologies such as video conference and online learning platforms, the online-driven model is likely to be how schools will operate in the future. In this kind of blended learning, traditional face-to-face, physical classroom teaching is advantageous to online teaching. Students do all their homework remotely, and teachers can send messages asking questions or solving problems online.

2.3   The Applications of B-Learning

Recent years, these novel patterns of B-Learning have been widely used in education domain and academia. Table 1 gives a review of blended learning for existing patterns. We review the related works by objectives, findings and patterns.

3   The Contrastive Analysis of Multiple Learning Mode

Rather than traditional learning mode and online learning mode, B-Learning has different concerns in learning mode and method. The differences feature in locations, learning approaches, technology use, flexibility, sense of participation, interaction and evaluation. The comparative features can be seen in Table 2.

For locations, traditional learning requires that students should be in physical classes, however, online learning and B-Learning allows the students in anywhere. B-Learning and online learning has more flexible location requirements. Also for learning approaches, traditional learning focuses on Face-to-Face mode, online learning uses the digital platform to accomplish the teaching, B-Learning can support Face-to-Face and Online, it has relative advantages in learning methods. Further, the technology is not necessary for traditional learning, but online

Table 1. Review of blended learning via using existing patterns

Author	Objectives	Findings	Patterns
Said et al. [6]	Learning computer programming	The data collected suggests that online conversations don't play a key role in programming	Face-to-Face Driver
Wang et al. [22]	Chinese university EFL Learning	An analysis of students' responses reveals that the blended design can create an efficient EFL learning environment and gain positive learner perceptions	Rotation
Berga et al. [3]	Explore undergraduate nursing health assessment course	For students in the blended course, perceptions of the online learning environment were positive.	Face-to-Face Driver
Polhun et al. [12]	Providing appropriate methodological guidance during the lockdown conditions	Moodle testing can be one of the most effective means of ultimately controlling students' knowledge	Online Driver
Kundu et al. [9]	Math and literacy learning	The blended learning atmosphere increases the classroom participation of students in elementary school classrooms	Rotation
Stanislaus [17]	Communication theology learning	These positive results show that the shepherds of the Catholic Church of the future can effectively integrate information and communication technology (ICT) into their lives and missions	Online Lab
Ariawan et al. [1]	Video on science learning outcomes	Video-assisted flex model learning has an impact on scientific Learning outcomes of ecosystem materials	Flex
Asadchih et al. [2]	Japanese oral language teaching for future philologists	The method can improve the level of competence in listening skill, monologue and dialogue speech	Face-to-Face Driver, Rotation, Flex Model, Self-Blend, Online Lab
Syakur et al. [19]	Reading English Learning	Online learning through the media learning can be effectively included in students' high response, improving students' scores and students' attitudes towards change and learning innovation	Online Driver
Tebbs et al. [20]	Developing specialty-nursing practice	Blended learning strategies play a role in enabling nurses to create their professional identity, find their place in the clinical team and meet the requirements of the organization	Rotation

learning use digital technologies to support the learning, B-Learning emphasizes the conjointion of digital technologies and offline teaching.

Regarding to the flexibility of learning, B-Learning and online learning has relatively much better effect on the teaching. But for pure online learning, it is unbenefit for sense of participation and interaction of students. Delialioglu et al. [4] claim that online-only has many problems, such as limited hardware, software, time, money, and teaching issues. There has been a new idea of combining the benefits of face-to-face courses with those of online courses to form the B-Learning model. Finally, for the evaluation, traditional learning is to test the students via offline exam. The manner is quite singleness, online learning can use the digital methods to test, but it is not comprehensive compared with B-Learning.

Table 2. The comparative analysis of B-Learning and traditional learning and online learning

Main features	Traditional learning	Online learning	B-Learning
Locations	Physical classes	Anywhere	Physical or Anywhere
Learning Approaches	Face-to-Face	Online	Face-to-Face or Online
Technology Use	No obligation for technology use	Use the digital technologies	Use the digital technologies
Flexibility	Bad	Good	Good
Sense of Participation	Good	Bad	Good
Interaction	Good	Bad	Good
Evaluation	Offline Exam	Online Test	Blended Evaluation

4   The Optimizing Strategies of B-Learning

Although the B-Learning has recieved intensive attentions in multiple domains, there are still various challenges in online resources, teaching methods, curriculum limitations, etc. Based on review the existing B-Learning works, we present the optimizing strategies as follows.

4.1   Using Intelligent Technologies Augment Teacher Preparations

For the actual B-Learning, there are existing that teaching resources are single, low independent of students' learning, lack of combination between classroom teaching and online learning. The development of artificial intelligence(AI) technologies, such as neural network, machine learning and emotional computing, not only provides new technical means to solve the above problems, but also promotes the further development of personalized, accurate and intelligent teaching toward the learner-centered direction. By using these new technologies, interaction and sense of participation for B-Learning can be further improved. Typically technical applications are given as follows:

Intelligent Evaluation. Intelligence assessment refers to a large-scale autonomous intelligence assessment based on the learning process and learning behavior data of learners and personalized immediate feedback. Among them, large-scale evaluation refers to the targeted evaluation of students' learning behaviors and learning outcomes through AI and big data analysis technology. Personalized instant feedback refers to giving feedback after analyzing the learning behavior and learning process data of a certain group of students. At present, the application of intelligent evaluation based on AI technology mainly includes speaking examiner and examination paper correcting robot.

As is known to all, there are various types of English listening and speaking tests every year. If the recording of the examinees is scored manually, it is not only a huge workload, but also difficult to maintain a unified evaluation standard. With the continuous improvement of speech recognition accuracy, it has become a reality to use AI speaking examiners to score English listening and speaking tests. By simply taking sample data and training them, AI speaking examiners can learn to evaluate students' responses in the same way as human examiners. In USA, some institutions had employed automated scoring of speaking for K-12 English language [5]. Also the automated speaking test in China had been used in National College Entrance Examination based on speech recogntion technologies [23].

Intelligent QA. Intelligent QA is an automatic response system of large-scale knowledge processing and feedback based on natural language processing, knowledge reasoning, text speech and image analysis. It mainly answers learners' questions from semantic understanding and answer search. For example: Microsoft xiaobing chat robot, Baidu intelligent question answering robot, they receive text, image or voice message, first to interpret the content, and then automatically give the appropriate responses.

In B-Learning, learners complete learning and teacher-student interaction through online and offline. According to the text, speech and image sent by learners, the AI teaching response robot based on deep learning, machine learning, neural network and other technologies can just show their talents. For example, Swathilakshmi et al. [18] has presented Student Suite+ which is a closed domain question answering system for educational domain, it can understand text and perform tasks like language translation and classifying a topic. Mathew et al. [13] has developed a personal learning assistant for school education based on NLP technologies.

Personalized Teaching. Individualized intelligent recommendation of teaching resources and individualized teaching according to students' personality characteristics has always been an ideal education method expected by the educational circles, but it is difficult to implement in detail. Personalized recommendation is to automatically predict the interests and preferences of learners according to their learning behaviors and push appropriate teaching resources to learners. Therefore, a large number of recommendation algorithms based on learning behavior data modeling have been applied, such as association rules algorithm, ant colony clustering algorithm, collaborative concern algorithm, machine learning algorithm, etc. Among them, deep learning recommendation algorithm based on artificial intelligence is the most concerned.

The idea of deep learning comes from machine learning. It refers to the process of data preprocessing, feature extraction and selection, inference and finally prediction after initial data acquisition. In hybrid teaching, feature extraction is carried out according to learners' behavior data of browsing text, voice, image, video and other resources on the Internet, and deep learning recommendation algorithm based on AI can provide learners with intelligent recommendation of learning resources. For example, intelligent recommendation and tutoring based on social network [21], a machine learning framework for English education [24], online course recommendation via machine learning algorithm [25].

4.2 Building Customized Learning Experience

To improve the customized learning experience of B-Learning, three critical factors should be concerned in actual teaching process.

Participation. The key to improve participation of students is strengthening the subject status of students. Strengthening the subject status of students lies in enhancing the self-efficacy of students in learning feeling and intrinsic value because students who think learning with others is useful are more likely to succeed to complete the task of cooperative learning. Also, they tend to have more faith in their own abilities. In addition, students who had positive beliefs about cooperative learning (i.e. interest and importance) were more likely to give a positive evaluation of the tasks involved in cooperative learning.

Immersiveness. The immersiveness of learning content is also a critical factor for customized learning experience. We should advocate that problem-solving driven learning process. Students are not passive knowledge receivers, but active information processors. On the network platform learning, students are guided to reflect on their knowledge and learning process, which can enhance their independent thinking, teamwork, selection, processing and the ability to create knowledge. But before the formation of the students autonomous learning awareness and habits, the supervision and guidance of teachers is indispensable. Teachers teach by asking questions, guiding, learning activities help students to step into the track of autonomous learning as soon as possible, wake up students' self-development awareness, and make students form a good view of learning.

Penetrability. The third critical factor is penetrability of learning effects. Five types of strategies should be utilized to guarantee the learning effects. They are monitoring and feedback strategy, online interaction strategy, collaborative learning strategy, level-based instruction strategy and multiple evaluation strategy. Monitoring is a kind of negative incentive. Blended learning provides students with a space for autonomous learning. Teachers expect students to complete their learning goals independently under the state of unmonitored, but it does not mean that students can learn by self-control, teachers should carry out necessary monitoring according to the feedback. Blended learning environment includes teacher-student interaction, student-student interaction, teacher-student and resource interaction. The interaction should pay attention to the quality and pursue the timeliness, rather than just a formal, random and blind interaction, but should consider the purpose of the interaction, the specific content of the interaction, the creation of the interaction opportunity and the impact of the interaction results on learning. Collaborative learning strategy is all related behaviors that students cooperate and help each other in order to achieve common learning goals and maximize individual and others' learning outcomes under certain incentive mechanism. Level-based instruction strategy requires that design learning tasks in layers. In learning tasks and teaching requirements to be differentiated, but also to facilitate hierarchical guidance of students. For example, students' level should be considered in the design of learning tasks, including basic tasks, ordinary tasks and improved tasks.

5 Conclusion

In this paper, we comprehensively survey the state-of-the-art works of B-Learning, specifically, the contation and types of B-Learning have been presented, and the main six patterns of B-Learning have been given in details. Furthermore, we give existing applications of these patterns in related domain. Subsequently, we offer the comparitive analysis the features of B-Learning and traditional learning and online learning. Finally optimizing strategies of B-Learning are discussed in detail.

Acknowledgements. This research was supported by Research on the Practice of Online and Offline Blended Teaching (No. SZIIT2021SK035), Research on the High Quality Development of Shenzhen Industrial System Under the New Development Pattern of Double Cycle (No. SZIIT2021SK010)

References

1. Ariawan, S., Aji, A.B., Tawil, T.: Pengaruh blended learning flex model berbantuan media video terhadap hasil belajar ipa materi ekosistem. Borobudur Educ. Rev. **1**(01), 44–56 (2021)
2. Asadchih, O., Dybska, T.: The experimental testing of blended learning methods of oral Japanese language teaching aimed at future philologists. ScienceRise Pedagogical Educ. **3**(36), 58–61 (2020)
3. Berga, K.A., et al.: Blended learning versus face-to-face learning in an undergraduate nursing health assessment course: a quasi-experimental study. Nurse Educ. Today **96**, 104622 (2021)
4. Delialioglu, O., Yildirim, Z.: Students' perceptions on effective dimensions of interactive learning in a blended learning environment. J. Educ. Technol. Soc. **10**(2), 133–146 (2007)
5. Evanini, K., Hauck, M.C., Hakuta, K.: Approaches to automated scoring of speaking for k-12 English language proficiency assessments. ETS Res. Rep. Ser. **2017**(1), 1–11 (2017)
6. Hadjerrouit, S., et al.: Towards a blended learning model for teaching and learning computer programming: a case study. Inform. Educ. Int. J. **7**(2), 181–210 (2008)

7. He, K.: New development of educational technology theory from blending learning. E-education Research (2004)
8. Hofraann, J.: Blended learning case study [eb/ol]. http://www.insynctraining.com/pages/blendedcasestudy.pdf
9. Kundu, A., Bej, T., Rice, M.: Time to engage: implementing math and literacy blended learning routines in an Indian elementary classroom. Educ. Inf. Technol. **26**(1), 1201–1220 (2021)
10. Li, J.: About the definition of blended learning. http://www.jeast.ne/jiahou/axehives/000618.html
11. Li, K., Zhao, J.: Principles and application modes of blended learning. e-Education Res. **07**, 1–6 (2004)
12. Lockee, B.B.: Shifting digital, shifting context: (re)considering teacher professional development for online and blended learning in the COVID-19 era. Educ. Technol. Res. Dev. **69**(1), 17–20 (2021)
13. Mathew, A.N., Paulose, J., et al.: NLP-based personal learning assistant for school education. Int. J. Electr. Comput. Eng. (2088–8708) **11**, 4522–4530 (2021)
14. Orey, M.: Definition of blended learning. University of Georgi, 21 February 2003 (2002)
15. Rao, V.: Blended learning: a new hybrid teaching methodology. Online Submission **3**, 1–6 (2019)
16. Singh, H., Reed, C., et al.: A white paper: achieving success with blended learning. Centra Softw. **1**, 1–11 (2001)
17. Stanislaus, I.: Forming digital shepherds of the church: evaluating participation and satisfaction of blended learning course on communication theology. Interact. Technol. Smart Educ. **19**, 58–74 (2021)
18. Swathilakshmi, V., et al.: Student suite+, a closed domain question answering system for educational domain. Turk. J. Comput. Math. Educ. (TURCOMAT) **12**(10), 3168–3172 (2021)
19. Syakur, A., Fanani, Z., Ahmadi, R.: The effectiveness of reading English learning process based on blended learning through "absyak" website media in higher education. Bp. Int. Res. Critics Linguist. Educ. (BirLE) J. **3**(2), 763–772 (2020)
20. Tebbs, O., Hutchinson, A., Lau, R., Botti, M.: Evaluation of a blended learning approach to developing specialty-nursing practice. An exploratory descriptive qualitative study. Nurse Educ. Today **98**, 104663 (2021)
21. Troussas, C., Krouska, A., Alepis, E., Virvou, M.: Intelligent and adaptive tutoring through a social network for higher education. New Rev. Hypermedia Multimedia **26**(3-4), 1–30 (2021)
22. Wang, N., Chen, J., Tai, M., Zhang, J.: Blended learning for Chinese university EFL learners: learning environment and learner perceptions. Comput. Assist. Lang. Learn. **34**(3), 297–323 (2021)
23. Wi, S., Wu, K., Zhu, B., Wang, S.: Voice assessment technology helps oral English teaching and evaluation. AI View **3**, 72–79 (2019)
24. Zhang, L.: A new machine learning framework for effective evaluation of English education. Int. J. Emerg. Technol. Learn. **16**(12) (2021)
25. Zhao, L., Pan, Z.: Research on online course recommendation model based on improved collaborative filtering algorithm. In: 2021 IEEE 6th International Conference on Cloud Computing and Big Data Analytics (ICCCBDA), pp. 437–440. IEEE (2021)

Research on the New Model of ShenShan Special Cooperation Zone of Shenzhen Coordinated Development of Regional Economy

Jinhong Xu[✉] and Yi Li

ShenZhen Institute of Information Technology, ShenZhen 517000, China

Abstract. after more than 40 years of reform and opening up, Chinese economic development has made remarkable achievements, but the imbalance of regional economic development is still prominent, which restricts Chinese long-term economic and social development. The central and local governments urgently need to explore a feasible model or path to solve this problem. Taking Guangdong Province as an example, this paper analyzes the current situation of uncoordinated regional economic development, points out its new model to solve the problem of uncoordinated regional economic development, empirically analyzes the relationship between institutional innovation and regional economic growth in the new development model, and based on the current development of ShenShan Special Cooperation Zone, discusses the innovation and demonstration value of "enclave" economic development model of ShenShan Special Cooperation Zone in promoting regional coordinated development, in order to provide demonstration and reference for China to solve the problem of regional development imbalance.

Keywords: Regional economy · Coordinated development · New model · ShenShan special cooperation zone

1 Raising of the Problem

After the reform and opening up, China's eastern coastal areas took the lead in realizing "going global" and became the pioneer of China's opening up. Global capital and cheap labor force in mainland China are constantly combined in the eastern coastal areas. In addition, China's vast territory, and the phenomenon of factor flow, especially the flow of labor force, is seriously divided among provinces, With the spatial agglomeration of economic activities, the difference of economic level between regions is increasing day by day. This kind of regional economic difference in China is mainly reflected in the rapid development of coastal cities, while the development of inland cities lags behind. This regional disharmony is also still obvious within a province.

Fund Project: ShenZhen Institute of information technology, school level doctoral program of Social Sciences–Research on the high quality development of ShenZhen industrial system under the new development pattern of double cycle, SZIIT2021SK010.

For a long time, China's central government and provincial and municipal governments have been committed to solving the problem of regional development imbalance. The 19th National Congress of China proposed to "establish a more effective new mechanism for regional coordinated development", raising the strategic guidance of regional coordinated development to a new level. Under the background of this strategic requirement and the current situation of uncoordinated regional development in Guangdong Province, this paper focuses on the innovative solution model - enclave economy adopted by Guangdong provincial government and Shenzhen municipal government to solve the problem of uncoordinated regional development. The development model of ShenShan Special Cooperation Zone has been changed several times, and finally becomes the "10 + 1" zone of Shenzhen, under the comprehensive management of Shenzhen, so it's important to explore the demonstration role and reference value of the development model of ShenShan Special Cooperation Zone to China's regional coordinated development.

2 Current Situation of Uncoordinated Regional Economic Development in Guangdong Province

As the most powerful province in China's economy, Guangdong's GDP reached 9.73 trillion yuan in 2018, but it also faces serious problems of regional development disharmony: the huge gap between the Pearl River Delta and Eastern and Northern and Western Guangdong is a long-standing problem in Guangdong's economic and social development, and it is also the biggest challenge to achieve the goals of "Three Orientations" and "two pioneers"[1].

2.1 Large Absolute Gap in GDP

Since the reform and opening up, the relative gap between the Pearl River Delta and Eastern, Western and Northern Guangdong has been narrowing, but the absolute gap is still widening. In 2008, the difference between the GDP of the Pearl River Delta and that of Eastern, Western and Northern Guangdong was 2269.3 billion yuan. In 2017, the difference between the two widened to 5646.5 billion yuan. Although the share of GDP of Eastern, Western and Northern Guangdong in the whole province has gradually increased since 2008, the Pearl River delta still plays a leading role. In 2008, the GDP of Eastern, Western and Northern Guangdong accounted for 19.1% of the total GDP of the province; In 2017, Eastern, Western and northern Guangdong accounted for 20.3% of the province's GDP, an increase of only 1.2% points over the past decade (Table 1).

---

[1] Guangdong should strive to become a vanguard in developing socialism with Chinese characteristics, a pioneer in deepening reform and opening up, a pilot area for exploring scientific development, and strive to take the lead in building a well-off society in an all-round way and basically realizing socialist modernization.

Table 1. Comparison of GDP of the Pearl River Delta and Eastern, Western and Northern Guangdong in 2007 and 2017

Region/proportion	2008	2017
GDP of Pearl River Delta (100 million yuan)	29745	75810
Proportion of GDP in the Pearl River Delta in the province's GDP (%)	80.9	79.7
GDP of Eastern, Western and Northern Guangdong (100 million yuan)	7052	19345
Proportion of GDP of Eastern, Western and northern Guangdong in the province's GDP (%)	19.1	20.3
GDP gap between the Pearl River Delta and Eastern, Western and northern Guangdong (100 million yuan)	22693	56465

2.2 Uncoordinated Development of Regional Industrial Structure

In 2008, the structure of the primary, secondary and tertiary industries in the Pearl River Delta was 2.4:50.3:47.3 respectively, adjusted to 2.0:45.3:52.7 in 2013 and 4.2:43.0:52.8 in 2017. The proportion of the tertiary industry continued to increase and the proportion of the primary and secondary industries decreased, which was in line with the industrial structure level of developed countries. The proportion of primary, secondary and tertiary industries in eastern Guangdong was 9.8:54.1:36.1 in 2008 and 7.6:52.2:40.2 in 2017; The proportion of three industries in western Guangdong was 21.2:43.4:35.4 in 2008 and 17.3:39.9:42.8 in 2017; The proportion of three industries in northern Guangdong was 17.0:50.4:32.6 in 2008 and adjusted to 15.1:37.5:47.4 in 2017. In contrast, the industrial structure of Eastern, Western and northern Guangdong is dominated by the primary and secondary industries, and the proportion of the tertiary industry still has great room for development.

2.3 There is a Big Gap in the Role of Central Cities

In the Pearl River Delta, Guangzhou, Shenzhen and other central cities have a prominent core position and radiation role. There are 12 cities in eastern Guangdong, western Guangdong and northern Guangdong, but there is no central city with special radiation capacity. The central city status in their respective regions is not prominent, and the energy to drive the overall regional GDP growth is relatively limited. In 2017, the total GDP of Shantou in eastern Guangdong was 235.076 billion yuan and that of Jieyang was 215.143 billion yuan; Shantou's per capita GDP is 42025 yuan and Chaozhou's per capita GDP is 40555 yuan. Shantou's advantages and driving role as a central city are not obvious. In 2017, the total economic output of Zhanjiang in western Guangdong was close to that of Maoming. The total GDP of Maoming was 292.421 billion yuan and that of Zhanjiang was 272.403 billion yuan. In addition, there is no significant difference between the two cities in the main indicators such as industrial added value, fixed asset investment, consumption, fiscal revenue and expenditure and people's per capita disposable income. In the mountainous area of northern Guangdong, the total economic output of Shaoguan and Qingyuan is close. In 2017, the total GDP of Shaoguan was 133.8 billion yuan, and that of Qingyuan was slightly higher than that of Shaoguan, with a total GDP of 155.09 billion yuan. Shaoguan cannot form an economic leader to radiate the surrounding areas.

2.4 The Income Gap Between Residents is Large

The relatively backward development of rural economy and the low income level of rural residents are also an important symbol of the imbalance of regional development in Guangdong. In 2007, the rural per capita net income was 5624 yuan, only 31.8% of the per capita disposable income of urban residents; Rural per capita consumption expenditure is 4202.32 yuan, only 29.3% of that of urban residents. In 2007, rural per capita net income increased by 6.4 times compared with 1978, only 17.3% of the real growth rate of GDP. In 2017, the income of rural residents in Guangdong Province was only 38.5% of the disposable income of urban residents. The income gap between residents in the Pearl River Delta and Eastern, Western and northern Guangdong is large. In 2017, the per capita disposable income of residents in eastern, Western and northern Guangdong was less than half of that in the Pearl River Delta. In October 2018, general secretary Xi Jinping pointed out in the speech at the end of the inspection work of Guangdong Province: "the imbalance between urban and rural development is the most prominent short board for Guangdong's development, mainly due to the relatively backward rural development in eastern Guangdong, western Guangdong and northern Guangdong. Guangdong has 446 thousand provinces to set a relatively poor population."

3 Exploration on the New Model of Coordinated Development of Regional Economy in Guangdong

The problem of uncoordinated regional development has become one of the prominent contradictions in China's social development in the new era, which seriously restricts the steady development of China's economy and even affects the harmony and stability of society. The central authorities have continuously launched strategic measures to promote coordinated regional development, and encouraged all regions to emancipate their minds and actively explore new ways. On May 12, 2017, the national development and Reform Commission, the Ministry of land and resources, the Ministry of environmental protection, the Ministry of Commerce, the General Administration of customs, the State Administration for Industry and commerce, the General Administration of quality supervision, inspection and quarantine and the Bureau of Statistics jointly issued "the guiding opinions on supporting the development of enclave economy", clearly supporting the development of "enclave economy" to solve the problems of uncoordinated regional development.

The Central Committee has always attached great importance to the coordinated regional development of Guangdong. The CPC Guangdong Provincial Committee and provincial government have also keenly grasped the unbalanced and insufficient economic and social development of Guangdong, adopted scientific planning, innovated systems and policies, and gathered all forces to promote the coordinated regional development, which not only implements the strategic deployment of the CPC Central Committee on coordinated regional development, Closely combined with the specific reality of Guangdong's regional development, it has constantly explored and practiced, actively practiced the central "enclave economy" strategy, first tried to establish the ShenShan Special Cooperation Zone, constantly adjusted the regional development mode, unremittingly innovated the management system and mechanism, and actively explored a new mode of regional coordinated Development - the enclave economy leading demonstration zone.

According to the idea of "enclave economy" management system classification, the mode evolution of the management system and mechanism of ShenShan Special cooperation zone can be roughly divided into five stages: multi-level subject participation mode, bilateral co management mode, flying out fully dominated transition mode, flying out fully dominated mode, and Leading demonstration area of "enclave economy". Among them, the overall leading mode of flying out is the final mode choice, which is the first in China and a pioneer in regional coordinated development and innovation.

3.1 Multi-level Subject Participation Mode

On May 21, 2011, the cooperation zone was officially established. The Party Working Committee and management committee are the dispatched offices of the Guangdong provincial Party committee and the provincial government. They entrust Shenzhen and Shanwei to jointly manage and exercise the management authority of prefecture level cities. At this stage, the management system and mechanism of the special cooperation zone belongs to the enclave economic model with the participation of multi-level subjects.

3.2 Co Management Mode

In December 2014, Shenzhen and Shanwei defined the division of role and the management authority of the cooperation zone between the two cities, gradually adjusted to Shenzhen leading economic construction, and Shanwei was responsible for land acquisition, demolition and social affairs. At this stage, the management system and mechanism of the cooperation zone belongs to the enclave economic model jointly managed by both flying out and flying in.

At the beginning of 2017, on the basis of summarizing the development experience over the years, the cooperation zone established the development concept of "relying on Shenzhen, linking Shanwei, based on ShenShan, and prospering the city through hard work", focused on giving full play to the main role of the Party Working Committee and Management Committee of the cooperation zone, paid close attention to the construction of industrial projects and fully promoted the infrastructure. This stage is a major decision and important period for the special cooperation zone to actively develop the regional comparative advantage of "enclave economy", undertake high gradient regional industrial transfer, stimulate endogenous growth momentum and strive to build a new growth pole under the joint management mode of both sides.

3.3 Flying Out Fully Dominates the Transition Mode

On April 7, 2017, Hu Chunhua, then member of the Political Bureau of the CPC Central Committee and Secretary of the Guangdong provincial Party committee, visited the special cooperation zone for the sixth time, listened to the report of the main leaders of the cooperation zone on the development and existing problems, and decided to transform the temporary and assistance management system into a long-term production, operation and management system.

On May 17, 2017, the office of Shanwei municipal Party committee issued "the emergency notice on relevant authority restrictions and asset freezing of EBu Town, Xiaomo Town, Chishi Town, Houmen town and Yuandun forest farm in Haifeng County", requiring that the relevant authority of "four towns and one farm" be restricted and relevant assets be frozen from May 17, 2017.

On September 21, 2017, the Guangdong provincial Party committee and the provincial government issued "the reply on the adjustment plan of the system and mechanism of the ShenShan Special Cooperation Zone". The cooperation zone was incorporated into the "10 + 1" district management system of Shenzhen, and comprehensive system and mechanism adjustment began from then on. In 2018, the Shenzhen Municipal Party committee and the Shenzhen municipal government issued "the work plan on the organization and implementation of the adjustment of the system and mechanism of the ShenShan Special Cooperation Zone", and determined the implementation plan for the adjustment of the system and mechanism of the cooperation zone. It can be said that since the freezing of relevant authorities and assets, the management system and mechanism of the cooperation zone began to enter the flying out leading transition period, and the promulgation of the two government documents made it clear.

3.4 Flying Out Fully Dominated Mode

In December 2018, the cooperation zone was officially quoted, the Party Working Committee and the management committee officially became the dispatched offices of the Shenzhen Municipal Party committee and the Shenzhen municipal government, and the special cooperation zone officially became the "10 + 1" District of Shenzhen. Since then, after the evolution of the "enclave economy" model, the cooperation zone has become an enclave dominated by one side with clear driving force, clear property rights and benefits, and full significance in operation, and officially entered the comprehensive leading period of the enclave.

3.5 Leading Demonstration Area of "Enclave Economy"

On August 18, 2019, "the opinions of the CPC Central Committee and the State Council on supporting Shenzhen in building a leading demonstration zone of socialism with Chinese characteristics" pointed out that it is necessary to "innovate, improve, explore and promote the management system and mechanism of ShenShan Special Cooperation Zone". This is an important symbol of the upgrading of the cooperation zone from a pioneer in exploring regional coordinated development in Guangdong Province and an experimental field for promoting system and mechanism reform to a national strategy, and comprehensively opens the historical curtain of the special cooperation zone's construction of a leading demonstration zone of socialist "enclave economy" with Chinese characteristics.

4   An Empirical Test on the Development Model of ShenShan Special Cooperation Zone and Regional Economic Growth

4.1   Selection of Important Institutional Factors

The innovation of management system and mechanism can be quantitatively studied through institutional variables. In the quantitative research on the impact of institutions on long-term economic growth, Song Deyong (1999) believes that industrialization, marketization and internationalization are important factors affecting China's long-term economic growth. Wang Wenbo, Chen Changbing and Xu Haiyan (2002) used principal component analysis to synthesize several kinds of institutional factors, such as property right system change, marketization degree, distribution pattern and opening to the outside world. Shen Kunrong (2002) analyzed the level of non nationalization, the degree of economic development, the degree of marketization and the pattern of economic benefit distribution, and obtained its impact on economic development. Fu Xiaoxia and Wu Lixue (2003) believe that marketization and opening to the outside world have a great impact on long-term economic growth. Ma Lijun (2010) believes that there are five types of institutional factors: property rights, openness, national effectiveness, industrialization and binary contrast coefficient. On the basis of previous research results, combined with the specific situation of the development of the cooperation zone, this paper selects two kinds of indicators: government effectiveness index and industrialization index to synthesize institutional proxy variables. Among them,

$$\text{Government effectiveness index} = (\text{GDP-General budget income} - \text{Government fund income})/\text{GDP} \tag{1}$$

$$\text{Industrialization index} = (\text{GDP-the first industry production})/\text{GDP} \tag{2}$$

4.2   Synthesis of Institutional Proxy Variables

In this paper, principal component analysis is used to synthesize institutional proxy variables. All data are from the internal statistics of relevant departments of the ShenShan special Cooperation Zone Management Committee. The sample interval is 2013–2019, of which the data of 2019 is the estimated value calculated according to the data of the first half of the year. Firstly, dimensionless GDP and time series of various institutional indicators are used, and then principal component analysis is carried out on different institutional variables using dimensionless data. The statistical information results are shown in Table 2 below.

Table 2. Statistical information of principal components

Principal component	Characteristic root	Contribution rate %	Cumulative contribution rate %
1	1.670	83.513	83.513
2	0.330	16.487	100.000

As can be seen from Table 2, the characteristic root of the first principal component is 1.670, which explains 83.513% of the total variance of the two original variables, more than 80%, so one principal component should be selected.

The comprehensive influence degree is calculated according to the component matrix and the variance of the extracted principal components:

$$\text{Comprehensive influence degree } Z = 0.835\text{PRIN} \tag{3}$$

$$Y_i = \sum_{j=1}^{2} \text{PRIN}_j \times Z \tag{4}$$

According to the above formula, the component coefficient is 0.547, i.e.

Institutional proxy variable I = 0.547 Government effectiveness index + 0.547 Industrialization index
$$\tag{5}$$

4.3   Econometric Test and Result Analysis of Institutional Factors in Economic Growth of ShenShan Special Cooperation Zone

4.3.1 Model Basis
Cobb Douglas production function is the model basis. It is derived by introducing the factor of technical resources in the form of general production function. The basic expression is as follows:

$$Y = f(A, K, L) = AK^{\alpha}L^{\beta} \tag{6}$$

Where Y represents output, A represents technological progress, K represents capital input (expressed by fixed asset investment in this paper), L represents the number of labor force, α, β represent capital and labor output elasticity respectively.

4.3.2 Model Extension
According to the actual situation of ShenShan special cooperation zone, its technological progress is mainly promoted by the administrative force of the government. The relationship between the two is as follows:

$$A = A_0 I^{\lambda} \tag{7}$$

Substitute Eq. (7) into Eq. (6) to obtain:

$$Y = A_0 I^{\lambda} K^{\alpha} L^{\beta} \tag{8}$$

Log the selected data to eliminate heterosexuality:

$$\ln Y = \ln A_0 + \lambda \ln I + \alpha \ln K + \beta \ln L \tag{9}$$

Table 3. Unit root test results

Variable	T statistical value	P value
GDP	−93.21531***	0.0001
I	−3.022576**	0.0174
K	−3.34107**	0.0124
L	−4.464931***	0.0048

Note: *means rejecting the original hypothesis at the significance level of 10%, **means rejecting the original hypothesis at the significance level of 5%, and ***means rejecting the original hypothesis at the significance level of 1%.

4.3.3 Regression Analysis

Before regression analysis, unit root test is needed to verify the stationarity of time series. After logarithmicization, ADF (Augmented Dickey-Fuller) method is used for unit root test (the results are shown in Table 3).

It can be seen from Table 3 that under the significance level of 5%, all the original sequences reject the original hypothesis, so it is considered that the original sequence is stable and can be subject to regression analysis. The regression results are shown in Table 4.

Table 4. Regression results of parameters

Variable	Coefficient	T statistical value	P value
lnK	0.468485***	45.0882	0.0000
lnL	0.117685***	5.0264	0.0000
lnI	0.089671***	−4.1614	0.0001
C	4.629968***	3.0998	0.0027

Note: *means rejecting the original hypothesis at the significance level of 10%, **means rejecting the original hypothesis at the significance level of 5%, and ***means rejecting the original hypothesis at the significance level of 1%.

It can be seen from the calculation results in Table 4 that capital, labor and institutional variables have a positive role in promoting the economic development of the cooperation zone, but the role of system is relatively small compared with the promotion of capital and labor, which is basically consistent with the reality that the ShenShan special cooperation zone is still in the initial stage of urban construction of large-scale development and construction, In a longer period of time in the future, the innovation of management system and mechanism will have a greater impetus to the economy of ShenShan special cooperation zone.

4.3.4 Causality Test

In order to test the existence and direction of the causal relationship between institutional proxy variable I and GDP, it is also necessary to conduct Granger causality test on the selected time series. According to AIC criteria, the lag order is selected as 2, and the test results are shown in Table 5.

Table 5. Granger causality test between institutional proxy variable I and GDP

Original hypothesis	F value	P value
GDP change is not the Granger cause of I change	2.06296	0.0521
I change is not the Granger cause of GDP change	3.87874	0.0368

It can be seen from the research results in Table 5 that under the confidence level of 10%, when it lags behind for 2 periods, institutional change is the Granger cause of economic growth, and economic growth is also the Granger cause of institutional change.

Through the above econometric analysis, we can draw the following conclusions: on the one hand, the adjustment of management system and mechanism plays a positive role in promoting its economic growth. After the comprehensive adjustment of the management system and mechanism of the special cooperation zone to Shenzhen at the end of 2018, the regional GDP reached 3670.74 million yuan in the first half of 2019, a year-on-year increase of 30.3%. This verifies the measurement results from the practical level: the adjustment of the system and mechanism of the cooperation zone has a great positive incentive effect on the market and driven the rapid growth of the regional economy. On the other hand, the economic growth of the cooperation zone is also an important thrust for the adjustment of management system and mechanism. In 2017, comrade Chan Yaodong, who was then the director of the Management Committee of the cooperation zone, adhered to the struggle thought of "get a place only when you work hard" and "looking up to the stars and walking down to the earth" and "focusing on EBu town, focusing on industry" when the management system and mechanism of ShenShan special cooperation zone were in the mode of joint management by both parties and faced many difficulties, Vigorously promote the economic construction of the cooperation zone and impress Secretary Hu Chunhua who came to ShenShan special cooperation zone for the sixth time with the actual achievements of economic growth. Secretary Hu Chunhua fully affirmed the investment attraction quality and development achievements of the cooperation zone, and personally guided and promoted the adjustment of the management system and mechanism of ShenShan special cooperation zone: the ShenShan special cooperation zone must be adjusted from the temporary and assistance system and mechanism to the long-term production, operation and management system and mechanism. The ShenShan special cooperation zone must be fully dominated by Shenzhen and become an important functional zone of Shenzhen. Thus, with the major decision-making and full support of the superior leaders, the ShenShan Special Cooperation Zone finally entered a new era of "enclave economy" development.

5   Innovation of Regional Coordinated Development Model of "Enclave Economy" in ShenShan Special Cooperation Zone

5.1   Create a Comprehensive Management System Dominated by the "Flying Out" Side

Solve the problem of poor management system and mechanism caused by the traditional "enclave economy" dominated by "flying in" one side or "flying in" and "flying out" two sides, and innovate the internal dynamic mechanism of "enclave" cooperation.

First, standardize the setting of management structure. In accordance with the unified deployment of the Guangdong provincial Party committee and the provincial government, actively promote the transformation of ShenShan special cooperation zone into an agency dispatched by the Shenzhen Municipal Party committee and the Shenzhen municipal government. The establishment of institutions and cadres and personnel refer to the setting of Shenzhen Economic Functional Zone, coordinate the entry of various state organs and functional departments, and change the "four towns and one forest field" under its jurisdiction into a street according to the relevant provisions of administrative divisions and adjustment procedures. Second, actively allocate the talent team, sort out and set the staffing, carry out personnel selection and recruitment, and speed up the staffing. Third, establish and improve the system, speed up the promulgation of "the regulations on the development of ShenShan Special Cooperation Zone", clarify the matters related to the adjustment of the system and mechanism of ShenShan Special cooperation zone in the form of legislation, and solve the common problems of "enclave economy", such as subject qualification, management authority, authorization mode, application of law, legal relief and so on. Pay close attention to the system construction, establish and improve the major system construction of ShenShan Special cooperation zone. Fourth, realize the unity of economic and social management. Integrate the cooperation zone into Shenzhen's national economic and social development system, implement regional government investment projects according to Shenzhen standards, and be fully responsible for the basic public services and social management of ShenShan Special cooperation zone. Fifth, clarify the interest sharing mechanism. Clarify the interest sharing of the "enclave" in terms of GDP, finance and taxation. During the internal assessment of the government, Shenzhen and Shanwei can include the GDP of ShenShan Special cooperation zone; Before 2020, Shenzhen and Shanwei will not participate in the fiscal and tax sharing of ShenShan Special cooperation zone, and all will be left to ShenShan Special cooperation zone. The fiscal and tax sharing scheme will be studied after 2021.

5.2   Initiate the Development Path of "Flying In" Side to Build a New City

Throughout the country, most of the existing "enclaves" are industrial parks with small area and single function. But ShenShan Special cooperation zone, the "enclave" economy is established according to the scale, function and organizational system of a new city, so it can be called a special zone in China's "enclave". Now, ShenShan Special cooperation zone should strive to be the "initiator of China's enclave economic development model, enclave governance model and enclave rural urbanization practice". Such exploration and initiative will provide valuable, replicable, popularized and exemplary experience for the national "enclave economy" development strategy.

According to the development idea of "planning leading, foundation first, platform driving and industry city integration", the first is high-point planning. Prepare the master plan with high starting point and high quality, and integrate the plan of ShenShan Special cooperation zone and the five-year development plan into the national economic and social development plan of Shenzhen. Second, accelerate the infrastructure construction of ShenShan Special cooperation zone. Formulate the overall urban road traffic plan to plan and build the internal and external communication framework of the cooperation zone; Rapidly promote the construction of backbone road network, and take the basically connected municipal road network as the power for subsequent urban construction; Create an intelligent transportation system, promote grass-roots infrastructure construction at full speed, strive to make up for the shortcomings of residents' living infrastructure, improve the level of basic public services, and make the development achievements cover more residents quickly and with high quality. Improve industrial supporting facilities, government service environment and industrial support policies, optimize the business environment, and make every effort to attract investment and talents. Third, forge the soul of high-quality development of the cooperation zone through various platforms, such as robot Town, cultural tourism town, Health and recovery Town, rebuilding grass-roots governance order and building a cooperation culture platform. Fourth, take the development path of "industry city integration". Gather various factors of production and basically build a more systematic and complete modern industrial system. The whole ShenShan Special cooperation zone "enclave" economy includes five group. The Eastern Group will build a Science and Education and Research zone and future industrial zone, the Southern Group will build an emerging seaport business district and coastal Ecotourism Zone, the western group will build an advanced manufacturing cluster, the northern group will build a health resort, and the central group will build a high-end business district and government affairs district, carry out urban functional planning and construction of comprehensive supporting facilities according to the standard of 3 million people, build supporting systems for public services such as education, medical treatment and culture, and lay the foundation for a quality life in the city.

5.3 Innovate the Dynamic Mechanism of Balancing Municipal Forces and Win-Win Cooperation Among Multiple Subjects

First, pay attention to giving play to the dual forces of the market and the government. The development of Special cooperation zone always depends on the dual forces of the government and the market. At each stage, the structure and role of the two forces are adjusted according to the actual situation. At the initial stage, the driving force of development was mainly government forces, especially the main driving force of Guangdong provincial Party committee and provincial government, which was later transformed into the joint promotion of government forces of Shenzhen and Shanwei, supplemented by market forces; Due to unclear property rights, government forces are prone to "tragedy of Commons" at this stage of development. Therefore, the main leaders of ShenShan Special cooperation zone actively give play to market forces, focus on EBu and industry, impress the provincial Party committee and government and Shenzhen Municipal Party committee and government with their achievements, and finally leverage government forces with market forces to successfully promote the transition and transformation of system and mechanism. At present, the development dynamic mechanism of ShenShan Special cooperation zone is mainly promoted by the government of Shenzhen, and the market force gives full play to the basic role of resource allocation. Second, continuously innovate the win-win cooperation mechanism. Focus on giving full play to the comparative advantages of all parties to achieve win-win cooperation. In the initial stage, the three-tier management mechanism, sound coordination mechanism and regular joint meetings were used to make high-level decisions, give full play to the comparative advantages of Shenzhen and Shanwei, optimize and innovate the system and mechanism while stabilizing the basic framework scheme, and form a co construction mechanism with reasonable division of labor and efficient operation. In the later stage, by establishing and improving the internal governance mechanism including the division of rights and responsibilities, the distribution of cooperative income, equal consultation and dispute resolution, the advantages of the system are used to make up for the problems that are difficult to solve in the exploration of the two places, so as to achieve the game balance of multi subjects in the "enclave economy" cooperation and consolidate the sustainable development of special cooperation.

6 Demonstration Value of "Enclave Economy" Development Model of ShenShan Special Cooperation Zone

6.1 Make a Demonstration on Innovating the Development Model of "Enclave Economy" and Poverty Alleviation Model

In essence, enclave economy is the asset reorganization of market elements in different spatial layout and the industrial reconstruction of value chain under the condition of existing administrative divisions. It tries to break through the regional economy and urban corporatism, reconstruct the region and coordinate the development between regions. From this perspective, enclave economy is a special phenomenon in the current national space reconstruction and a flexible experimental means to reconstruct the relationship between fields under the original institutional framework. Enclave economy should be matched with other spatial or non spatial policies, play a more important role in national spatial reconstruction, and provide a platform for deeper inter city cooperation.

It is an important choice for China to solve the regional imbalance of economic development and realize complementary advantages, resources and factors among different regions. From the perspective of national strategy, the exploration of ShenShan Special Cooperation Zone will provide valuable experience for the country to develop enclave economy.

After ShenShan Special cooperation zone was listed as the dispatched office of Shenzhen Municipal Party committee and government on December 16, 2018, it was upgraded from version 4.0 of urbanization targeted poverty alleviation to version 5.0 of the new poverty alleviation model of "rebuilding a new city"[2], that is, a modern international coastal smart new city completely dominated by Shenzhen, a leading demonstration area of socialism with Chinese characteristics, a developed place, with Shenzhen as the benchmark, high-quality planning, high-quality construction and high-quality development. For the national poverty alleviation, it means opening up a new and higher-level idea, which plays a subversive innovation demonstration and leading role.

6.2   Make a Demonstration on the Path of Innovative Regional Coordinated Development

The exploration of Enclave Economy in ShenShan Special Cooperation Zone has contributed to improving the balance and coordination of development in Guangdong and turning the short board into a "potential board". The development of Enclave Economy in the cooperation zone will not only realize the rapid economic development in ShenShan Special cooperation zone, but also become the fulcrum of Shanwei's take-off. Especially after Guangdong Hong Kong Macao Big Bay area has become a national strategy, ShenShan Special cooperation zone, as the eastern portal of Guangdong Hong Kong Macao Bay area, is an important fulcrum for the eastward expansion and radiation of the core cities of the bay area, It is a new growth pole driving the development of eastern Guangdong.

The fourth meeting of the 12th Guangdong provincial Party committee clearly put forward that Guangdong Province should focus on building the regional development pattern of "one core, one belt and one area" and accelerate the coordinated development of regions. ShenShan Special Cooperation Zone is an important link closely connecting the core area of the Pearl River Delta, the coastal economic belt and the northern Ecological Development Zone, with obvious regional advantages. The enclave economic development of ShenShan Special cooperation zone can make full use of the functional transfer of regional industries, form a high-level division of labor and cooperation, cultivate and form a new growth power, effectively enhance the development potential of eastern and northwestern Guangdong, expand the new development space of the Pearl River Delta, and make a demonstration in promoting the balanced development of Guangdong Province.

For Guangdong, the exploration and development of the enclave economy of the cooperation zone is a reform exploration of strong decentralization and an attempt of a new urbanization construction mode. Shenzhen is encouraged to give full play to the spirit of the special zone of daring to break through and try, being the first and working hard, practice the new development concept on the white paper "enclave" of the cooperation zone, build an industrial new city with high standards, and drive the development of Shanwei, Feed back the old revolutionary base areas, explore a new model for the revitalization and development of East and northwest Guangdong, explore a new road for the coordinated development of national regions, and provide a new sample of Guangdong regional coordinated development.

---

[2] Shenzhen's poverty alleviation in Shanwei has experienced version 1.0 of money and materials, version 2.0 of poverty alleviation, version 3.0 of industrial transfer park, version 4.0 of targeted poverty alleviation and targeted poverty alleviation to "rebuilding a city" through cooperation Poverty alleviation version 5.0 has five stages.

The experience of the ShenShan Special Cooperation Zone in the past seven years is a problem-solving process of continuous reform and solving the problem of unbalanced economic development in Guangdong Province.

6.3 Make a Demonstration in Innovating a Mutually Beneficial and Win-Win Cooperation Model

ShenShan Special Cooperation Zone, a comprehensive management system and mechanism led by Shenzhen, has brought space for industrial expansion to Shenzhen, faster economic growth to Shanwei and new opportunities for the development of the two cities.

ShenShan Special Cooperation zone has become the "10 + 1" zone in Shenzhen. First, it means that Shenzhen has more industrial transform space. Through industrial co construction, it optimizes Shenzhen's industrial layout, promotes industrial transformation, upgrading and innovative development, and provides new support for Shenzhen to build a leading demonstration zone for high-quality development. At the same time, it also means that Shenzhen has transferred some urban functions to ShenShan Special cooperation zone in an orderly manner, and has a new urban space to provide citizens with more people's livelihood and well-being; Secondly, for Shanwei, it also means multiple profits. First, we can strengthen ties with Shenzhen, including industrial chain supporting, transportation interconnection and personnel exchanges, so as to better integrate into the Pearl River Delta; Second, if the economic development of ShenShan Special cooperation zone is good, the radiation capacity is enhanced, and the "cake" is bigger, Shanwei can better share economic achievements, including industrial co construction and tax sharing; Third, it can give play to its territorial and geographical advantages and enjoy the medical, educational and other urban services of ShenShan Special cooperation zone nearby; Fourth, it provides a new communication platform. Cadres in Shanwei can exercise in ShenShan Special cooperation zone nearby and learn from the development experience of Shenzhen more conveniently.

The release of "The opinions of the CPC Central Committee and the State Council on supporting Shenzhen in building a leading demonstration area of socialism with Chinese characteristics" has ushered in new historical development opportunities for Shenzhen. As the "10 + 1" District of Shenzhen, ShenShan Special cooperation zone also stands at a new starting point for the development of "enclave economy", and has also made important exploration and demonstration for the new model of regional coordinated development.

References

1. Chan, Y.: Research on the development of ShenShan Special Cooperation Zone from the perspective of "enclave economy" model. China Spec. Econ. Zone Res. (00), 137–151 (2018)
2. Wang, J., Liu, Z.: Research on development ideas of ShenShan Special Cooperation Zone. Spec. Econ. Zone (01), 19–22 (2019)
3. Yu, D.: Research on enclave economic model and its mutual benefit and win-win mechanism. Theoret. Observ. (07), 78–80 (2019)

4. Ding, W.: Research on enclave economic development: a literature review. Economist (04), 55–57+102 (2019)
5. Zhang, Y.: Research on economic development strategy of enclaves in the Yangtze River Delta Based on industrial integration. Modern Econ. Inf. (01), 478 (2019)
6. Qi, X., Gu, J.: Enclave marriage between "special zone" and "old area" – exploring a new model of enclave economy from ShenShan Special Cooperation Zone. China Market (24), 24–25 (2018)
7. Qian, W.: Research on local government cooperation in the governance of "enclave economy" – taking ShenShan Special Cooperation Zone as an example. J. Xiamen Spec. Zone Party School (05), 40–47 (2017)
8. Wu, F.: "Enclave economy": a new system of regional cooperation and development. People (16), 11–13 (2017)
9. Ma, B., Du, P.: Research on the governance of "enclave economy" in regional economic cooperation. J. Tianjin Inst. Admin. 16(02), 71–79 (2014)
10. Feng, Y.: Research on enclave economic model and its mutual benefit and win-win mechanism. Res. Financial Issues (07), 94–102 (2013)
11. Chen, J., Jia, L.: Solving the bottleneck of development with "enclave economy." Zhejiang Econ. (06), 14–15 (2012)
12. Yin, J.: Thoughts on the development of "enclave economy" in Henan Province. J. Henan Inst. Financial Manage. Cadres 26(06), 118–121 (2008)

Design of IoT Health Pension Scheme Based on Physiological and Behavioral Indicators for Elderly

Quan Yuan[1], Mao Li[1(✉)], Rui Zhou[1], Hu Su[1], Hao Feng[1], Jing Wang[1], Xuejiao Pang[1], Siyao Wang[1], Tianlei Zhang[1], and Xiaohu Fan[1,2]

[1] Department of Information Engineering, Wuhan Collage, Wuhan 430212, China
{19202130109,19202030106,19202030123,19202130107, 18202030107}@mail.whxy.edu.cn, {9315,8206,8335,9452, 9420}@whxy.edu.cn
[2] PIESAT International Information Technology Co. Ltd., Beijing, China

Abstract. In recent years, the health and safety problems of the elderly increase continuously, coupled with the age of information technology, the elderly are difficult to adapt to the society, so the use of modern Internet technology to protect the health and personal safety of the elderly, has become a top priority. Therefore, this paper, based on the Internet of Things technology, mainly monitors the elderly's indoor behavior, supplemented by the monitoring of physiological indicators, outdoor behavioral trajectories and falls, proposes the Internet of Things health pension scheme design based on the physiological and behavioral indicators of the elderly. This scheme involved the minimum confidence interval solution strategy, according to the old people in different parts of the activity rate for the elderly indoor dwell time detection, and combined with travel anomaly detection algorithm, pulse wave signal analysis algorithm, fall detection algorithm and other algorithms, real-time monitoring of physiological indexes of elders trajectory data and behavior, the guardian and the hospital can check at any time, once the old man has an accident. The system will send abnormal information to the monitoring system of WeChat mini program guardian and community hospital in time, and the corresponding personnel will immediately take treatment measures to ensure the health and safety of the elderly. This system combines the health and safety problems of the elderly to consider the possible accidents, from monitoring, prevention and treatment, the elderly, children and the hospital are closely linked together, to ensure the health and safety of the elderly to provide a comprehensive solution.

Keywords: Internet of Things · Elderly care · Health services · Behavior recognition

1 Introduction

As of March 2020, China had 904 million Internet users and 64.5% Internet penetration rate, but only 6.7% of Internet users aged 60 or above, according to a statistical report on China's Internet Development [1]. According to 2019 data from the National Bureau of

A. Katangur and L.-J. Zhang (Eds.): SCC 2021, LNCS 12995, pp. 59–73, 2022.
https://doi.org/10.1007/978-3-030-96566-2_5

Statistics, the population aged 60 and above was 264.02 million, accounting for 18.70% (5.44% points higher than 2010), of which only 23% were online [2]. From these two data, there are hundreds of millions of elderly people failed to take the information express in time. With the acceleration of China's aging process, the development of the pension industry has risen to the level of national strategy. Three out of four people have never been connected to the Internet. As a result, nearly 80% of seniors still don't use smartphone apps, which have emerged in recent years, to get health care.

According to the research results on major e-commerce platforms, most of the products are wearable measurement products for home use. For example, electronic blood pressure meter with wrist can measure blood pressure and heart rate. Although all of these products, such as aging and testing speed technology already quite mature, but most of the elderly daily monitoring products of single function and low cost performance, especially the drawback is that the product does not automatically and body do comprehensive analysis, combined with other physiological indexes for the elderly to provide reliable comprehensive proposals to improve the body. For the guardians, the measured physical indicators cannot be fed back to the guardians in real time, so that the health and personal safety of the elderly living alone can not be guaranteed, and will increase the worry of the guardians in other places.

2 Related Work

In order to better understand the difficulties in the life of the elderly and enhance the feasibility of the design of health pension plan, this paper adopts the method of random sampling to conduct a questionnaire survey on 268 empty nesters living in the community to understand the needs of the elderly for remote care, and analyzes the data based on the Kano model [3]. Chi-square goodness of fit test showed significant differences between the actual and expected quantities of each item of tele-care needs ($P < 0.01$), indicating that the samples had specific personal preferences for the Kano category. The expectation degree of tele-nursing service was 48.37%–80.86%, the satisfaction degree was 57.09%–67.56%, and the dissatisfaction degree was 11.92%–37.93%. Programs such as Remote One-click Emergency Calling and Remote Emergency Assistance Arrangements were perceived by empty-nesters as one-dimensional qualities, while the rest were attractive qualities. In the quadrant analysis chart, all tele-care services were classified as attractive quality [4]. Therefore, according to this demand, questionnaire survey is adopted to deeply analyze the needs of the elderly for daily living facilities and the measures that guardians can take to ensure the personal safety of the elderly, so as to put forward a feasible and practical health pension plan.

It includes research on users' behavior habits, thinking habits, user needs, etc., demand analysis, weight ratio analysis according to the importance degree, and detailed scheme design, so that the design results conform to the behavior habits and thinking habits of the elderly and guardians, to achieve the desired effect (Fig. 1 and Table 1).

2.1 Analysis of Survey Results

Based on the analysis of the above research results, we need to design products that conform to the physical characteristics, thinking habits and behavior habits of the elderly

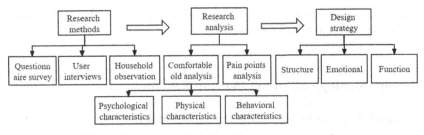

Fig. 1. Research method of intelligent endowment plan

Table 1. Basic information of residents

Project	Grouping	Number of persons (n)	Percentage (%)
Living situation	Living alone	199	36.5
	Many people live with	346	63.4
Chronic diseases	Hypertension	283	51.9
	Coronary heart disease	103	18.9
	Diabetes	191	35.0
	Other	133	24.4
	There is no	117	21.5
Ability to care for	Fully care	203	37.2
	Some care	155	28.4
	Cannot provide for oneself	187	34.3

when designing smart pension programs. For the needs of the elderly and their guardians, this paper extracts the following needs as the focus, and constructs a smart pension plan.

Physical Sign Parameter Detection. The elderly are faced with many chronic diseases. Long-term monitoring of basic physical parameters is beneficial to the discovery and treatment of diseases.

Human Posture Detection. The elderly group will bring many problems due to the change of physical state, especially the occurrence of falling, which will cause great harm to the crowd and is a big trouble in the daily life of the elderly group. In the elderly group, the elderly who live alone and are widowed are more likely to cause irreparable injuries due to falls. Therefore, it is important for older people to recognize falls and get treatment at the earliest opportunity.

Wireless Network Choice. The choice of wireless communication technology, the elderly group generally has a small range of outdoor activities, activities are generally in communities and other places close to home, and the activity level is relatively low. Secondly, most of the elderly have limited knowledge and learning level of mobile phones and other smart electronic products. Therefore, it is particularly important to choose the right wireless communication technology and remove the shackles between mobile phones and monitoring equipment.

3   Design Strategy of Smart Pension Scheme

3.1   Overall Program Design of Monitoring Equipment

After analyzing the target group of the elderly, the system needs to have the following functions, as shown in Fig. 2 and the overall process, as shown in Fig. 3:

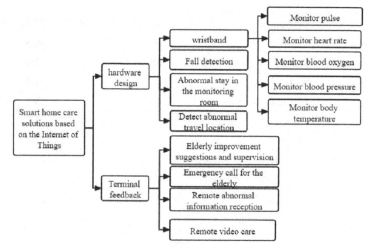

Fig. 2. Overall function design diagram

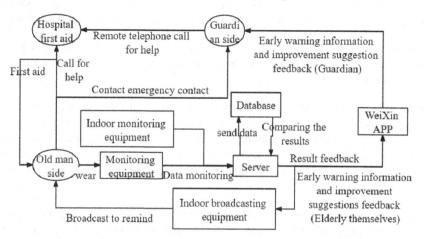

Fig. 3. Flow chart of roles and functions of smart pension plan

3.2   Functional Overall Design

Function Total Hardware Design. The monitoring equipment can detect vital signs such as pulse, body temperature, heart rate, blood oxygen and blood pressure, as well as monitor the three behaviors of falling, staying and traveling, so as to complete the monitoring of the elderly in many aspects. The overall flow chart of monitoring equipment software design is shown in Fig. 4.

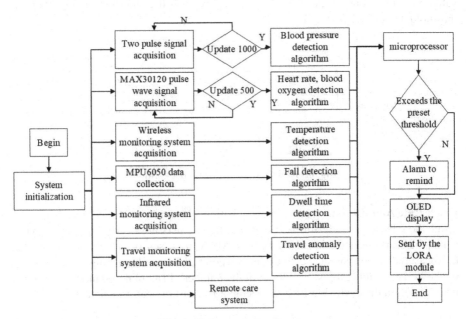

Fig. 4. Software design drawing

Pulse Wave Signal Acquisition and Data Feature Point Extraction. Pulse wave signal analysis and processing algorithm reference, pulse wave signal analysis and processing implementation [5]. In this system, MAX30102 integrated chip and Pulse Sensor are selected as the pulse wave acquisition terminal in the sign detection module. In this paper, the pulse wave sampling rate was set as 100 Hz, the LED pulse width was set as 411 μs, and the ADC full scale value was set as 4096 Therefore, PPG signal acquisition process of this module is shown in Fig. 5.

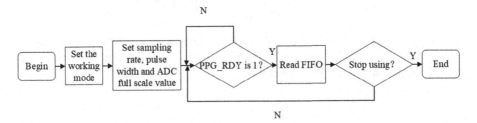

Fig. 5. Signal sampling flow chart

The recognition of pulse potter collection point detection algorithm flow chart shown in Fig. 6, the first after pretreatment of pulse wave signal is the same spacing of segmentation, and then in turn to each division signal processing, according to the first time window to estimate signal amplitude, by calculating the average time signal amplitude, and the value is defined as the threshold. Secondly, the first-order differential calculation of the signal is carried out. The sampling point before the zero-crossing of the first-order differential signal is judged to be positive and its amplitude is greater than the threshold value, then this point is the crest. If it is negative and the amplitude is less than the threshold, the point is a trough.

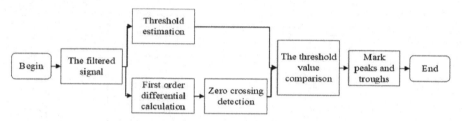

Fig. 6. Flow chart of recognition algorithm

Heart Rate Acquisition. Heart rate acquisition algorithm reference [6], heart rate acquisition: Heart rate refers to the number of times a person's heart beats at rest. In this paper, the heart rate detection module adopts MAX30102 sensor to obtain PPG signal of the measured object, and then extracts feature points through filtering algorithm. Finally, the heart rate is indirectly solved through the number of sampling points and sampling interval within the cycle. Figure 7 shows the flow chart of heart rate detection.

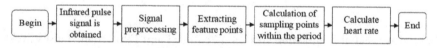

Fig. 7. Flow chart of heart rate acquisition

Blood Oxygen Acquisition. Blood oxygen acquisition algorithm: Oxygen saturation is the ratio of oxygenated hemoglobin in blood to white blood red eggs. The calculation formula of blood oxygen is as follows:

$$SpO_2 = \left(\frac{C_{HbO_2}}{C_{HbO_2} + C_{Hb}} \right) \times 100\% \tag{1}$$

Where C_{HbO_2} is HbO_2 concentration, C_{Hb} is Hb concentration, and SpO_2 is blood oxygen value. In this paper, photoelectric volume pulse wave is also used to detect blood oxygen. The experimental data are shown in Table 2.

Table 2. Blood oxygen calibration (partial data)

Serial number	1	2	3	4	5
System measures R value (10^{-4})	6436	5828	5902	6287	7286
Oxygen in YX301 (%)	96	98	98	97	94

According to the above experimental data, the calibration parameters are obtained through data fitting. The linear equation of data fitting is, and the determination coefficient is 0.9627. Therefore, there is a good fitting relationship between the R value measured by the system and the blood oxygen value measured by the oxime-ter $SpO_2 = -32.78 * R + 117.3$. In blood oxygen detection, the blood oxygen value can be calculated by calibration formula after R value is calculated, so as to realize continuous blood oxygen value monitoring.

The system uses two different light in MAX30102 sensor to obtain the corresponding PPG signal, and obtains the R value based on the calculation principle of blood oxygen saturation. The blood oxygen saturation value was obtained by the calibration formula. Figure 8 is the flow chart of blood oxygen saturation detection.

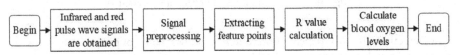

Fig. 8. Flow chart of obtaining oxygen saturation

Blood Pressure Acquisition. The blood pressure acquisition algorithm is based on pho-toelectric volume method of photoelectric sensor [4]. The system uses a PluseSensor analog sensor to detect two pulse waves and get the coordinate values of feature points after pretreatment. The pulse wave conduction time can be obtained by multiplying the average difference of the calculated feature points within the period with the sampling rate, which is set as 100 Hz in this paper. Finally, blood pressure was obtained by the formula calibrated by different individuals. Figure 9 is the flow chart of blood pressure detection.

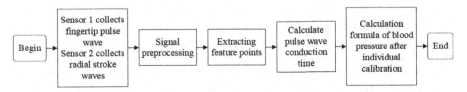

Fig. 9. Flow chart of blood pressure acquisition

Body Temperature Acquisition. Body temperature is obtained using a wireless health monitoring system that measures core body temperature [5]. The system, invented by Wei et al., uses high-precision sensors, low-power MCU and multi-channel ISM band

RF (RADIO frequency) method. It is composed of wireless temperature measurement equipment and receiver equipment. The device measures skin temperature from a person's back to monitor core body temperature. When used, the wireless temperature measuring device is installed on the skin surface of the lower back of the neck. The receiver device is used to obtain data from the transmitter and send data to Want Want Health mini program. The elderly wear the sensor, and the temperature data monitored is transmitted to the remote data server for analysis and processing through the mobile communication network. Figure 10 is the flow chart of body temperature acquisition.

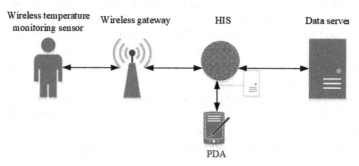

Fig. 10. Flow chart of body temperature acquisition

Fall Detection. In this paper, observation Windows and optimization features are obtained through the research of SVM based fall detection algorithm, which are used to guide the research of threshold analysis based fall detection algorithm, and finally realize real-time fall detection on terminal hardware [7]. The flow chart of fall detection based on literature is shown in Fig. 11.

Infrared Detection of Abnormal Residence Time in Indoor Space. Infrared monitoring system consists of five parts, including human infrared sensor, time and intermediate relay, transformer and warning lamp. The duration of entering the area was measured to determine whether the elderly were abnormal. The external human infrared sensor is installed at the door, used to detect whether there is someone in the door; The built-in human infrared sensor is installed inside the door to detect whether the elderly really enter the area, so as to avoid false positives caused by simple proximity.

In order to obtain the stay time range of the elderly at a key point under normal circumstances, the strategy in this paper is to select the minimum and maximum values from the daily time sample data obtained as the left and right boundaries of the stay time. Since the safety problems of the elderly are mainly related to long-term stay problems, this paper only studies long-term stay points. However, with the increase of sample data, many outliers appear in the sample data, which affects the accuracy of behavior analysis. In order to avoid such influence, considering that the residence time of the elderly in key areas in their daily activities meets the characteristics of normal distribution, the minimum confidence interval solution strategy is adopted in this paper to obtain the threshold range of residence time. Firstly, obtain the longest resident time of the elderly in a key point within a certain period of N consecutive days (N > 30), and regard it as

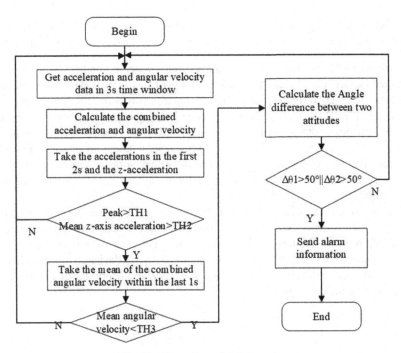

Fig. 11. Flow chart of fall detection

sample data, which are respectively denoted as $D_1, D_2, \ldots, D_N$. And calculate the mean value and standard deviation of sample data, as shown in Formula (2) and (3).

$$\overline{D} = \frac{1}{N} \sum_{i=1}^{N} D_i \tag{2}$$

$$S = \sqrt{\frac{1}{N-1} (D - \overline{D})^2} \tag{3}$$

Thus, the minimum confidence interval of residence time can be obtained as follows:

$$(D_{\min}, D_{\max}) = \left(\overline{D} - ta_{/2}(N-1)\frac{S}{\sqrt{N}}, \overline{D} + ta_{/2}(N-1)\frac{S}{\sqrt{N}} \right) \tag{4}$$

Where α is the confidence degree and $1 - \alpha$ is the confidence level. The greater the confidence level is, the more reliable the estimation result is. α are usually recommended 0.01, 0.05, or 0.1, with confidence levels $1 - \alpha$ of 0.99, 0.95 or 0.9. $ta_{/2}(N-1)$ is the upper quantile of t distribution with $N - 1$ degree of freedom about $a/2$, which can be obtained from the query table. $D_{\min}$ represents the left edge of the key dwell time, and $D_{\max}$ represents the right edge of the key dwell time.

The minimum confidence interval strategy can preliminarily judge the resident time range of the elderly's daily behavior. Considering that environment and regional sensitivity also affect the elderly's daily behavior, this paper added correlation coefficient and buffer coefficient on the basis of the minimum confidence interval to distinguish the influence of different environment and different sensitivity regions on residence time.

Correlation Coefficient. The behavior of users in the indoor environment is closely related to external factors, which mainly include the following aspects: season, weather, health, temperature, humidity, light and other indoor environmental factors. For these external factors, it is difficult to analyze the relationship between external factors and residence duration with clearly defined functions or data. In this paper, external factors of the same type are set $S = \{s_1, s_2, \cdots s_n\}$, where 'n' represents n situations of such factors, and then quantified into corresponding numbers according to the progressive relationship of their grades, and the size of the numbers represents the degree of influence on the resident time [6].

The literature regularizes seasonal factors and determines their fuzzy theory domain as [2, 4], which is converted into corresponding numbers according to the progressive relationship between the tempo of the old people's behavior rules in different seasons [7]. It is assumed that there is a certain correlation between the behavioral resident time of the same user in different seasons, and the calculation formula of the correlation coefficient is defined as follows:

$$R_{s_i}\left(s_j\right) = exp\left[-\frac{\left(s_j - s_i\right)^2}{\sum_{n=1}^{4} s_n}\right] \tag{5}$$

In the formula $R_{s_i}\left(s_j\right)$, represents the correlation coefficient between s_i season and s_j season. After the regional resident time interval is preliminarily calculated based on the minimum confidence interval, the degree of influence of external environmental factors on the behavioral resident time of the elderly is taken into account, and the correlation coefficient under the circumstances s_j is calculated by using Formula (6). The new confidence interval formula is as follows:

$$R_{s_i}\left(s_j\right) \times \left(D_{min}, D_{max}\right) = \left(R_{s_j}\left(s_j\right) \times D_{min}, R_{s_j}\left(s_j\right) \times D_{max}\right) \tag{6}$$

Buffer Coefficient. Different indoor areas have different degrees of sensitivity. Generally, indoor areas can be divided into two categories: sensitive area (toilet) and non-sensitive area (restaurant). Older people are more likely to have accidents in sensitive areas. In non-sensitive areas, older people are less likely to have accidents. Therefore, in order to control the sensitivity of the system, buffer coefficient should be set to distinguish the influence of different sensitive areas on the life of the elderly.

$$U = p \times l \tag{7}$$

In the above formula, U represents buffer, P represents buffer coefficient, and l represents confidence interval length. The length of the confidence interval can be calculated by the minimum confidence interval:

$$l = 2ta_{/2}(N - 1)\frac{S}{\sqrt{N}} \tag{8}$$

The smaller the buffer coefficient P is, the higher the warning sensitivity of the system is. In sensitive areas, there is a high probability of danger for the elderly. If the buffer coefficient is set to be small for timely warning, the setting range of P is 0.05–0.2. In non-sensitive areas, the buffer coefficient is set to be large so as not to affect life, generally set to 0.2–0.5 [5]. Add the buffer to the confidence interval formula and get Eq. (9):

$$\left(\overline{D}_{\min}, \overline{D}_{\max}\right) = \left(\overline{D} - ta_{/2}(N-1)\frac{S}{\sqrt{N}} - U, \overline{D} + ta_{/2}(N-1)\frac{S}{\sqrt{N}} + U\right) \quad (9)$$

On the basis of the correlation coefficient already considered, the new confidence interval is added to form the minimum confidence interval based on the correlation coefficient and buffer coefficient:

$$\left(D_{\min}^*, D_{\max}^*\right) = \left(R_{s_i}\left(s_j\right) \times \overline{D}_{\min}, R_{s_j}\left(s_j\right) \times \overline{D}_{\max}\right) \quad (10)$$

Using the correlation coefficient and buffer coefficient discussed above, a new confidence interval is formed $\left(D_{\min}^*, D_{\max}^*\right)$. When the resident time of the elderly at a key point is within the range $\left(D_{\min}^*, D_{\max}^*\right)$, the key point is identified as the stop point. According to experience, it takes less than 2 s to cross a certain point when walking. When the time at a certain point is less than 2 s, it proves that the old man did not stay. In view of the difference in the range of different indoor key points and the mobility and walking speed of different elderly people, positive offset Y was added on the basis of 2 s to form a new threshold value without stopping T_{th}, and the behavior below T_{th} was judged as a non-stopping behavior. When the duration of time in an area exceeds the specified warning time, the system will alert with a light on, as shown in Fig. 12.

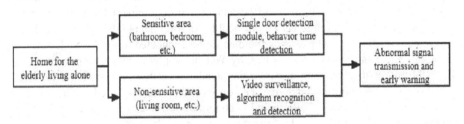

Fig. 12. Infrared monitoring process scheme

Abnormal Travel Location Monitoring. Abnormal travel location is a common problem among the elderly, so it is necessary to monitor the abnormal travel location of the elderly. For denoising and segmentation of the original track data of the elderly, this paper adopts track segmentation based on safety area [8]. The process is shown in Fig. 13. If there is any abnormality, inform the guardian of the wechat mini program terminal system.

Remote Care System. The main hardware of the remote monitoring system is the web camera. The camera Angle and signal transmission must be guaranteed when the network camera is placed, and the infrared monitoring system warning light can be viewed to avoid dead corners. Through the remote care system, children can monitor the activity status and track of the elderly in real time, digitize the collected data, and transmit it to the Wechat mini program of Want Want Health through the network. Guardians can

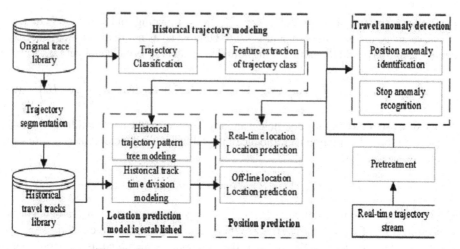

Fig. 13. Data processing and location monitoring process

combine the sensor monitoring data above to monitor the living conditions of the elderly in real time. If abnormal conditions are found, they can call the nearby community service agencies through the alarm system.

Test Item. The monitoring equipment transmits the collected data to the data receiving equipment. This paper adopts LoRa technology to realize the wireless transmission between the monitoring equipment and the data receiving equipment. Data after receiving device to receive data through HTTP protocol to transmit data to the system server, the server receives the data after storing the data to the connected to the MySQL database in this paper, using the prosperous healthy WeChat applet access system server, data from the server database and compare the standards set by the system range, If the value is within the normal range, the data only needs to be displayed on the interface of wechat applet terminal; If the value is abnormal, the micro program terminal will display abnormal indicators and inform the guardian to take corresponding measures in time. The block diagram of the system network layer is shown in Fig. 14.

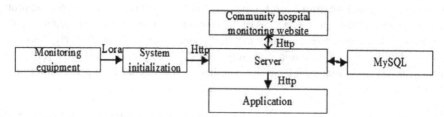

Fig. 14. Block diagram of system network layer

4 Case Study

The wechat applet is developed using languages such as WXML, WXSS, and JavaScript to provide remote status monitoring and emergency calls, as shown in Fig. 15(left). Meanwhile, the data of various physical indicators such as pulse, blood pressure, blood oxygen, heart rate and temperature can be obtained and displayed on the background server to monitor the changes of physiological indicators of the elderly, as shown in Fig. 15(middle), showing abnormal state monitoring. In addition, the location and movement track of the elderly can be displayed in real time, as shown in Fig. 15(right), and the historical records can be recorded and saved, which can be viewed at any time.

Fig. 15. Functional interface display, physiological abnormality monitoring and activity track interface

Table 3. The acceptance of the pension scheme survey (partial data)

	Options	Number of people	Percentage
Usage intention	Be willing to	242	90.3
	Be unwilling to do	26	9.7
	Price	188	70.1
Use focus areas	Functional utility	195	72.9
	Ease of use	93	34.8
	Privacy and Security	82	31.3

The results of the usability evaluation of this product are very impressive. When the questionnaire survey was conducted after the detailed introduction of our smart pension solution and products based on the Internet of Things for community residents, 88.1% of the users thought it was useful, easy to use and learn, and all the measured indicators were effective and comprehensive, which could effectively solve most problems in the life of the elderly. 90.3% expressed strong willingness to use the product, and the function and price of the product basically met their psychological expectations, but 39.7% of them remained skeptical about the experience of the product, expecting to have a physical experience. As shown in Table 3.

5 Summary and Discussion

5.1 Scheme Summary

This paper proposes an Internet of things health pension scheme based on the physiological and behavioral indicators of the elderly. This scheme has developed a complete set of monitoring and alarm schemes for the physical conditions, movements and activities of the elderly, so that all aspects of the elderly's life can be effectively monitored. Combined with medical monitoring platform (PC and APP) and small programs for medical staff and elderly relatives to achieve efficient health monitoring. The program consists of the following four parts.

Physiological Monitoring Scheme. The five basic physiological data of pulse, heart rate, blood oxygen, blood pressure and temperature are monitored in real time through the body detection device of the Internet of Things. When the data received by the device is returned to the database, abnormal information will be fed back in time to give a warning when compared with the normal data set by the system. Abnormal information will be notified to the children through wechat mini program terminal, and relatives will be reminded to send the elderly to medical treatment in time, so as to avoid missing the best treatment time.

Motion Monitoring Scheme. Through the fall detection equipment for the elderly to monitor the daily actions, the old man to make every action at the same time, the equipment of the sensor can get a set of real-time acceleration and angular velocity data back to the database, when a group of behavior data clearly beyond the set outside the scope of normal, judged to be falling state, by small program to send information to their children and hospital, quickly send medical first aid.

Indoor Activity Monitoring Program. Use monitoring equipment to directly check the living status of the elderly. If the elderly stay longer than normal, infrared monitoring equipment in the area of the red light will light up, while sending alarm information to the small program.

Outdoor Activity Monitoring Plan. Abnormal use travel position monitoring device for the old man's position, an abnormal travel time and travel outside the residence time abnormal monitoring early warning, through the process and track algorithm, determine whether the travel time and travel locations or residence time is unusual, if abnormal then send alarm information to the small program.

5.2 Future Perspectives

The program allows caregivers, the elderly and their families to be closely linked, and the physical condition and location information of the elderly can be shared in real time, ensuring the health and personal safety of the elderly and the peace of mind of the guardian. In the future, we plan to carry out long-term evaluation, constantly optimize and improve the equipment, and design and improve products based on the development concept of "people-oriented", so as to produce products with more perfect functions, more user-friendly and easy to wear.

References

1. Zhou, M., Sun, X., Huang, L.: Chronic disease and medical spending of Chinese elderly in rural region. Int. J. Qual. Health Care 33(1), mzaa142 (2020)
2. Kim, M., Chang, M., Nam, E., et al.: Fall characteristics among elderly populations in urban and rural areas in Korea. Medicine 99, e23106 (2020)
3. Sun, X., Yan, W., Zhou, H., et al.: Internet use and need for digital health technology among the elderly: a cross-sectional survey in China. BMC Public Health 20(1) (2020). Article number: 1386. https://doi.org/10.1186/s12889-020-09448-0
4. Yuan, Y., Liu, Y., Gong, L., et al.: Demand analysis of telenursing for community-dwelling empty-nest elderly based on the Kano model. Telemed. e-Health 27(4), 414–421 (2020)
5. Kyriakoulis, K., Kollias, A., Destounis, A., et al.: Detection of atrial fibrillation during routine 24-hour ambulatory blood pressure monitoring in the elderly: comparison with 24-hour electrocardiography. J. Hypertens. 36, 109–110 (2018)
6. Shi, Y., Yang, J., et al.: Research on wireless ecg monitoring system based on IoT technique. Basic Clin. Pharmacol. Toxicol. 118(1), 81–81 (2016)
7. Mrozek, D., Koczur, A., Maysiak-Mrozek, B.: Fall detection in older adults with mobile IoT devices and machine learning in the cloud and on the edge. Inf. Sci. 537(5), 132–147 (2020)
8. Boukhennoufa, I., Amira, A., Bensaali, F., Esfahani, S.S.: A novel gateway-based solution for remote elderly monitoring. J. Biomed. Inform. 109, 103521 (2020)
9. Juarez, J.M., Ochotorena, J.M., Campos, M., et al.: Spatiotemporal data visualisation for homecare monitoring of elderly people. Artif. Intell. Med. 65(2), 97–111 (2015)
10. Lupiani, E., Juarez, J.M., et al.: Monitoring elderly people at home with temporal case-based reasoning. Knowl.-Based Syst. 134, 116–134 (2017)
11. Obayashi, K., Masuyama, S.: Pilot and feasibility study on elderly support services using communicative robots and monitoring sensors integrated with cloud robotics. Clin. Ther. 42(2), 364–371 (2020)
12. Cappelleri, C., Janoschka, A., Berli, R., et al.: Twenty-four-hour ambulatory blood pressure monitoring in very elderly patients. Medicine 96(34), 7692 (2017)
13. Gill, A.Q., Phennel, N., Lane, D., et al.: IoT-enabled emergency information supply chain architecture for elderly people: the Australian context. Inf. Syst. 58, 75–86 (2016)
14. Varnfield, M., Jayasena, R., O'Dwyer, J., et al.: ISQUA16-2955 home telemonitoring for aged care – do the elderly comply and complete. Int. J. Qual. Health Care 28(suppl_1), 66–67 (2016)
15. Bicharra Garcia, A.C., Vivacqua, A.S., Sanchez-Pi, N., et al.: Crowd-based ambient assisted living to monitor the elderly's health outdoors. IEEE Softw. 34(6), 53–57 (2017)

Innovation of Teaching Mode of Comprehensive Engineering Cost Training Course Based on OBE Concept in the Era of Big Data

Huijie Jiang[1], Yuanzhi Wang[2], and Xiangbo Zhu[1(✉)]

[1] Shenzhen Polytechnic, Shenzhen 518055, Guangdong, People's Republic of China
zxb@szpt.edu.cn
[2] ShenZhen Dongsen Construction Project Management Co., Ltd., Shenzhen 518081, Guangdong, People's Republic of China

Abstract. This paper explores the teaching mode of practical training courses in higher vocational education, taking the engineering cost major as an example, with the functional advantages of Internet information technology and the concept of results-oriented education. In order to achieve effective docking between the demand of market positions for the comprehensive ability of professional students and the supply of colleges and universities for students' ability cultivation, that is, students can be employed after graduation, this paper rationally allocates the professional teaching program, teacher collocation, system management methods, etc., by applying the massive professional information resources of the Internet, the guidance advantages of offline school-enterprise teachers and the resource advantages of school-enterprise practical training.

Keywords: Big data · OBE concept · Engineering cost majors · Teaching mode

1 Overview

With the rapid development of Internet information technology, the combination of information technology and teaching pattern has given rise to new teaching modes, such as building information technology application in the project cost professional courses by 2D drawings data can not only make students learn 3D information, promote the student to the professional course in the practice of conceptual knowledge comprehension [1]. At the same time, it also improves the teaching efficiency and teaching quality of professional courses.

Especially the new champions league in 2020 during the epidemic prevention and control, the Internet information technology in higher vocational education has played a prominent role in the teaching, through the implementation of the "live online +" teaching model, at the same time of speeding up teaching keep up with the trend of the information age to ensure the progress of the higher vocational education teaching, and abundant information resource in the Internet also provides a wealth of knowledge reserves for the lectures [3]. Higher vocational education provides positive conditions for

A. Katangur and L.-J. Zhang (Eds.): SCC 2021, LNCS 12995, pp. 74–83, 2022.
https://doi.org/10.1007/978-3-030-96566-2_6

the training of high-tech talents in engineering cost specialty by relying on the information environment outside the course and combining with the integration of architectural model technology in the internal knowledge system of the course, and has important practical significance for promoting the development of modern construction enterprises [2]. In view of this, the team in the project cost professional "project cost comprehensive training courses as the research object, by Internet big data for the environment, results oriented education concept as the research train of thought, to explore the course of teaching mode innovation, in order to realize the effective docking between the cultivation of high and new technology talents and the employment demand of modern construction enterprises.

2 Research Idea

With the intensification of global competition and the shortening of product innovation cycle, the industrialization of construction market is developing faster and faster. The combination of knowledge economy and "product-oriented" production organization fits the development concept of modern vocational education system effectively. Under the influence of the market economy system, the implementation of the pilot work of modern apprenticeship has not only been supported by the policies of the national, provincial and ministerial government departments, but also been recognized by industry associations, enterprises and public institutions as well as the public [4, 5]. The development prospect of the modern apprenticeship talent training mode is bright. In this paper, by combining the ability of market position and the graduation requirements of the colleges and universities, the full use of the Internet under the background of big data online open course resources, with the course teaching is directly related to the construction of teachers team, professional quality training, course construction, evaluation and professional course completion standard pertinence analysis such as content, to further improve performance of the cultivation of the students, At the same time, promote the benign and sustainable development of modern apprenticeship pilot work.

As shown in Fig. 1, the advanced features and functions of engineering education curriculum reform at home and abroad are analyzed by means of conceptual analysis and literature research, so as to grasp the role of curriculum reform in the cultivation of skilled talents in higher vocational colleges and the problems to be solved [6, 7]. At the same time, combining with the demand characteristics of the post capacity in the cost market of our country and the graduation requirements of colleges and universities, this paper gives specific implementation suggestions on the reform of the comprehensive practical training courses of the engineering cost major in higher vocational education of our country.

3 Insufficiency of Curriculum Construction

3.1 The Relatively Weak Faculty in Practice

The essence of vocational education is to impart more scientific and rigorous knowledge and skills to students through the combination of theory and practice, but it is mostly

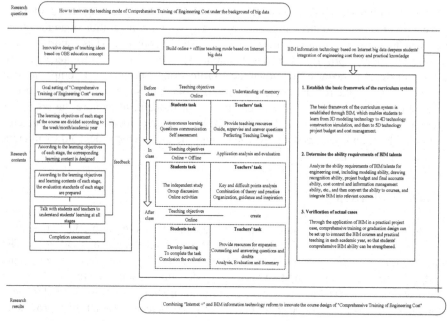

Fig. 1. Innovative design ideas of the course comprehensive training of engineering cost under the concept of OBE

limited to the general content of the major. The comprehensive practical training course of engineering cost focuses on the training of students' professional skills, which requires professional teachers with rich practical skills to give guidance and assist teachers in the practical analysis of theoretical knowledge within the course [8]. However, due to the lack of practical ability of school teachers and the lag of the update of professional equipment in school, they cannot guide students to acquire the characteristic knowledge and skills needed in practical posts.

With the increasing improvement of the living standard of the public, the cultivation of professional talents should not stay on the basis of "ordering" talent cultivation based on school-enterprise cooperation, but should strengthen the cooperative work between schools and enterprises, and give full play to the guidance advantages of schools and enterprises in mastering students' knowledge and skills. However, in the process of school-enterprise joint training, although enterprise teachers have enough professional practical skills, they will not be able to pour out the ink because they have not received systematic educational training. Therefore, in the process of the implementation of modern vocational education system, the primary task is to reserve a solid professional, practical and experienced team of double teachers.

3.2 Lack of Professional Quality of Fresh Graduates

With the concept of "Industry 4.0" proposed in Germany, China has also gradually started the intelligent process of industrial development. The implementation of this economic development mode needs the support of a large number of skilled and innovative talents, especially the emphasis on the professional qualities such as the craftsman's attitude of hard work and the talent being the only one. In the process of market visit and research, this paper found that enterprises pay more attention to the basic professional qualities of candidates when examining their comprehensive professional ability [9]. The focus of the project cost comprehensive training courses is to strengthen the training of the students' practical skills and professional quality, and also need to develop in the process of teaching students to think independently, the solution of the problem actively seek, teamwork and professionalism, this can not only help students in the face of the problems in the process of training to have strong psychological quality. At the same time, you can also get sustainable growth, that is, you can quickly adapt to the market speed when you enter the market position.

At the present stage, technical talents in China are gradually becoming younger. After they are retrained and able to undertake projects independently, they seek other employment opportunities because they are not satisfied with the current development status, which leads to the overall development trend of high mobility of employment in the market [10]. Although the flow of talents can promote the development of enterprises to a certain extent, a large amount of manpower and material resources invested in the training period are not sufficiently returned after the completion of the training, which will cause incalculable losses to enterprises. Therefore, in order to enhance the enthusiasm of enterprises to participate in the training of modern apprenticeship talents, the key is to strengthen the training of professional quality of knowledge and technology talents.

3.3 Relatively Weak Practical Courses

At present, the teaching materials used in vocational education are mostly borrowed from the undergraduate teaching materials, that is, the theoretical knowledge system is the main part, and the comprehensive practical training courses of engineering cost which mainly focus on practical skills are the same. Although the market demand for professional knowledge is taken into account in such curriculum setting, the teaching methods of professional practical skills are not fully considered. Moreover, the teaching methods are mostly cramming and instilling text, pictures, videos, etc., and the training of students' practical operation ability is still insufficient.

At present, the foundation of vocational education is relatively weak, excellent professional curriculum developers are relatively scarce, and the top-level structure of curriculum development is not perfect, thus leading to the failure to establish authoritative national vocational education teaching standards. With the rapid development of market demand, most vocational colleges begin to learn from foreign advanced teaching concepts, and visit the job demand of the domestic market, actively build in-school training bases, and carry out various forms of teaching reform, such as project teaching method, module teaching method, task-driven teaching method, independent teaching method. However, while learning from the teaching advantages of foreign countries, schools ignore their own teachers, equipment scale and the actual situation of foreign development, and the inspection of in-school practical training courses is mostly limited to students' general knowledge and skills, which leads to students' lack of sufficient professional ability in the face of market demand. Therefore, this kind of one-way communication teaching mode has been dissatisfied with the demand of vocational talent training, it is necessary to accelerate the innovation and reform of modern vocational education.

3.4 Relatively Single Form of Assessment

The implementation of student assessment is a favorable entry point for vocational education to cultivate students' knowledge ability, change teachers' evaluation concept and deepen school-enterprise cooperation, which plays a strong guiding role in achieving the goal of talent training, innovating curriculum content and improving the quality of school-enterprise cooperation. In order to improve the passing rate of students, vocational education at the present stage mostly simplifies the examination form of students and adopts the in-school examination based on the nature of standard answer, especially for the comprehensive practical training course of engineering cost which is based on the nature of practice. This form of assessment not only restricts the students' own spirit of innovation and divergence, but also its evaluation standards do not fit well with national technical standards and industrial standards.

At present, in addition to the provisions of the Vocational Education Law of the People's Republic of China on the system of academic certificates and vocational qualification certificates, there are relatively few legal norms and systems for students' academic evaluation, especially for the design of academic examinations, examination contents and scoring standards. At present, talent training focuses on the comprehensive professional qualities of students when they apply for enterprises, so the assessment and evaluation should not be limited to the identification of standard knowledge and skills. It is necessary to innovate and reform the evaluation standards of talent training, and increase the participation of enterprises, so as to improve the effectiveness and attractiveness of modern apprenticeship education.

4 Suggest Measures

Through market investigation and analysis, it is found that engineering cost professionals not only need to have enough professional knowledge, but also need to have skilled practical skills, psychological quality, team spirit and other professional qualities to deal with the practical problems of the project. The comprehensive practical training course of engineering cost, as the concentrated performance of the ability of cost professionals, should have enough teachers to guide the course during the teaching process, including the teaching of professional knowledge, the exercise of practical skills, the training of professional quality and the evaluation of professional courses. This process is in close agreement with the characteristics of "double tutor" and curriculum standard highlighted in the modern apprenticeship talent training mode.

4.1 "Double Mentor" Team Coordination

In the process of talent cultivation and implementation of modern vocational education, it is necessary to establish a team of "double tutors" with solid professional and rich practical experience.

On the one hand, enterprise teachers will play the role of educators in the talent training mode, just like school teachers. In this process, based on their high professional skills and good professional ethics, enterprise masters also need to master basic pedagogy knowledge including educational purpose, mentoring relationship view and skills learning rules, so as to be able to teach their skills to apprentices in an orderly and logical way. Then realize the apprentice training from unstructured development to structured development. In order to achieve this goal, enterprises can send young and middle-aged backbone teachers to schools to receive theoretical knowledge re-education. Moreover, in order to make teachers feel at ease to receive teaching guidance at school to improve their teaching level and fully integrate the knowledge learned into the professional practice teaching system, enterprises need to formulate corresponding management measures for dispatched teachers, and specify the time, treatment and assessment rules for teachers to study in school. At the same time, the school can also hire engineers or technical personnel working in the front line of the cooperative enterprises to guide teaching in the school, which can not only save the school funds, but also teach the latest professional development technology to the students. Through the above way of full-time or part-time teaching, it will be more conducive to ensure the quality of teaching and the continuous improvement of teachers' professional ability.

On the other hand, most vocational colleges require a master's degree or above when recruiting teachers. Although they have a high theoretical level, but because of the lack of enterprise practice link edification and experience, resulting in a relatively weak practical ability. In order to solve this problem, the school can select young and middle-aged backbone teachers to the production line of enterprises for on-the-job internship, and cultivate the engineering practice ability of professional teachers by learning the most cutting-edge new knowledge, new technology and new process in the industry. At the same time, in order to make teachers feel at ease to exercise and study in the enterprise and improve their consciousness to exercise in the cooperative enterprise, the school should formulate corresponding management measures for the dispatched teachers, so as to clarify the time, treatment and assessment rules for teachers to exercise in the enterprise.

4.2 The Craftsmanship of Professionalism

As the cradle of social applied talents, vocational education should pay equal attention to the cultivation of professional quality and craftsman attitude of would-be professionals (vocational students) as to the cultivation of professional knowledge and skills, no matter to meet the market demand or the individual development needs of students. In the training mode of modern apprenticeship, both schools and enterprises should play an important role in cultivating students'/apprentices' professional qualities.

On the one hand, enterprises cultivate the professional attitude of "apprentices" mainly from the three dimensions of professional career, role model and social psychology. The master teaches the apprentices by words and deeds through his own career experience and the personal charm of the craftsman masters around him, and gradually internalizes the "craftsman spirit" into the education process. And in the apprenticeship work, recognition and care gradually from the perspective of social psychology to improve students' enthusiasm and enthusiasm for work, while through the development of "apprenticeship" practice work norms to cultivate apprentices serious, responsible and assiduous work attitude.

On the other hand, vocational colleges enhance students' understanding of the "craftsman spirit" and cultivate their professional spirit of advocating work, loving work and devoting themselves by carrying out ideological and political moral quality education, organizing professional spirit practice education activities and carrying out special education of "personal deeds of advanced figures and model workers". After that, teachers help students analyze the demands of vocational positions on professional quality, and carry out task teaching or project teaching based on work. In this process, we should not only highlight the individual students' initiative to explore the practical process, but also integrate the craftsman spirit into the professional teaching objectives, so as to cultivate students' patient, careful, serious and responsible working attitude. After the students/apprentices pass the academic assessment and the company's internship inspection, the company will formally sign the contract with the outstanding apprentices.

4.3 Curriculum Standard and Post-Based

In view of the vocational education talent training process, the key to the effectiveness of teaching implementation is the need for schools and enterprises to coordinate the formulation of curriculum standards according to the talent training objectives. Through the combination of enterprise employment needs, post qualification standards, national vocational qualification standards and vocational students' cognitive laws, the typical work tasks corresponding to the major can be transformed into learning tasks, and then the original discipline knowledge system can be broken, and the construction goals and vocational ability goals of related courses can be defined.

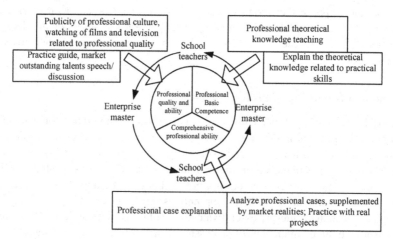

Fig. 2. The teaching content of the course involves

The results of comprehensive practical training courses of engineering cost, as the concentrated embodiment of the training of talents of cost specialty, need to strengthen the construction of three parts of professional quality ability, basic professional ability and comprehensive professional ability (as shown in Fig. 2) when the school and enterprise jointly build the course standard system. While clarifying their own curriculum division and job responsibilities, schools and enterprises will set curriculum standards, curriculum implementation plans and corresponding leading and follow-up courses according to curriculum requirements. Among them, for the part involving professional courses, the courses and practical training projects will be determined through school-enterprise consultation, and professional teaching standards and assessment and evaluation standards suitable for professional courses will be formulated. In this process, we should not only consider the analysis of the professional ability of the post, but also combine the growth rules of technical and skilled talents, the work content of the market post and the professional teaching content of the national professional qualification standard. Through this virtuous circle, which is led by the state, charged by higher vocational colleges and followed by enterprises, we hope to realize the modern apprenticeship system in the true sense, in which schools and enterprises jointly play the main responsibility of educating people.

4.4 Diversification of Assessment Standards

In order to reflect the effectiveness of the implementation of the modern apprenticeship talent education mode in the comprehensive practical training course of engineering cost, schools and enterprises need to jointly build a set of assessment and evaluation system for both theoretical and practical skills for this course, and evaluate the knowledge, skills and professional qualities that students/apprentices have mastered under this mode of education.

On the basis of the subject examination and student satisfaction survey commonly used in vocational colleges at the present stage, the evaluation of behavior layer and outcome layer should be increased, which should not only objectively reflect the improvement of student/apprentice practice ability, but also reflect the important role of apprenticeship education in the improvement of enterprise benefit. In order to play an important role in the training of technical and technical talents, modern apprenticeship system should not only judge the practice of students/apprentices by teachers according to the traditional mode of rating, but also emphasize the sense of responsibility of students in the practice process. Through daily feedback on teachers' teaching and communication between teachers and students on knowledge reception, the linkage between teachers and students can be strengthened, so as to promote students to effectively receive knowledge and improve teachers' teaching efficiency (as shown in Fig. 3).

4.5 Certificate of Completion Standard

It has been more than 20 years since the concept of modern apprenticeship was formally put forward in the UK in 1993, and now it has basically achieved leap-forward development of vocational education. The most important thing is that the training mode of modern apprenticeship in the UK has established close relationship with the national vocational qualifications. Apprenticeships gain qualifications that are not only recognized by employers across the country, but also link up with GCSE to further higher

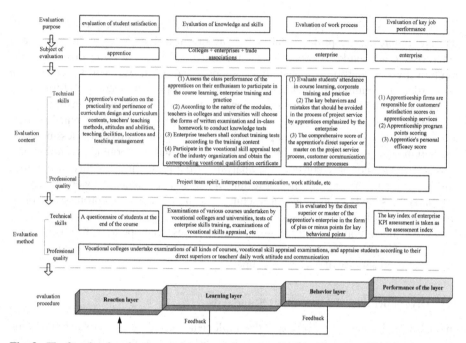

Fig. 3. The four-level evaluation model of modern apprenticeship. Note: Modified drawing based on Feng Xiaofei (2016).

education. Due to the characteristics of the development of China's basic national conditions, it is impossible to replace vocational qualification certificate and education certificate equally, but both of them should be taken into account simultaneously. Through the integration of professional education, general education and continuing education, a learning system of credit accumulation and transfer has been established. And promote the mutual recognition of educational achievements of various models, so as to break the ceiling restricting the training of technical personnel, and then provide students in need with the opportunity of continuing education, as well as the diversity of choices and the path of multi-path talent.

In the process of jointly formulating the assessment standards and procedures for professional quality and ability of posts, schools and enterprises should follow the following working principles: the assessment of enterprises is the priority, and the assessment of colleges is the auxiliary; Professional quality and skill assessment, theoretical knowledge examination as a supplement; The main work attitude and performance, regular examination as a supplement. The quality assessment and professional selection of students should be carried out jointly by schools and enterprises, so as to achieve both vocational skill certificates and graduation certificates at the same time.

5   Conclusion

The training goal of the practical course of engineering cost major is to cultivate talents of applied engineering technology, which should ensure the cultivation of college students' professional application ability and the improvement of their comprehensive quality. This study on the teaching mode of comprehensive practical training courses of engineering cost major embedding big data information technology and OBE education concept, through massive online professional information resource database and offline professional school and enterprise teachers. Furthermore, while effectively connecting the demand of market positions for students' comprehensive abilities with the cultivation of students' abilities by colleges and universities, the teaching scheme, teacher collocation, system and methods corresponding to the practical training courses should be reasonably allocated.

Acknowledgment. This work was supported by the 2018 Guangdong Higher Vocational Education Teaching Quality and Teaching Reform Engineering Education Teaching Reform Research and Practice Project (GDJG2019421), Shenzhen Educational Science 2020 Annual Planning Project (ybzz20008), Humanities and Social Sciences Annual Project of Shenzhen Polytechnic (No. 602930239), Humanities and Social Sciences Youth Project of Hubei Provincial Department of Education (No. 17Q056), Open fund project of Hubei Provincial Humanities and Social Sciences Key Research Base–Reservoir Immigration Research Center (No. 2016KF11).

References

1. Yang, L., Zeng, F., Yao, D.: Exploration on innovation education of higher vocational automobile specialty based on internet thinking. In: Liu, B., Jia, L., Qin, Y., Liu, Z., Diao, L., An, M. (eds.) EITRT 2019. LNEE, vol. 640, pp. 389–396. Springer, Singapore (2020). https://doi.org/10.1007/978-981-15-2914-6_37
2. Tasova, N.K.: New approaches in design and vocational education: impact of the internet design education and digitalize. Proc. Soc. Behav. Sci. **106**, 1905–1916 (2013)
3. Liu, J.: Research on the application of internet technology in teaching reform in higher vocational colleges. J. Phys. Conf. Series **1648**(2), 022129 (2020)
4. Sudira, P.: The role of vocational education in the era of industrial automation. J. Phys: Conf. Ser. **1273**(1), 012058 (2019)
5. Geng, H.: The innovation strategy of higher vocational students' education management guided by OBE concept. Int. J. New Develop. Educ. **2**(3), 58–61 (2020)
6. Lin, G., Bai, K., Kong, Z., Kong, L.: Improving innovation education for vocational college students by the OBE concept. Acad. J. Humanit. Soc. Sci. **1**(1), 102–106 (2018)
7. Prihantoro, C.R.: Vocational high school readiness for applying curriculum: outcome based education (OBE) in industrial 4.0 era. Int. J. Curriculum Inst. **12**(1), 251–267 (2020)
8. Luo, G.S.: An exploration of curriculum construction in higher vocational education with a working and learning combination pattern. In: Zhang, L., Zhang, C. (eds.) Engineering Education and Management. Lecture Notes in Electrical Engineering, vol. 111. Springer, Heidelberg (2012). https://doi.org/10.1007/978-3-642-24823-8_24
9. de Oliveira Silva, J.H., de Sousa Mendes, G.H., Ganga, G.M.D., Mergulhão, R.C., Lizarelli, F.L.: Antecedents and consequents of student satisfaction in higher technical-vocational education: evidence from Brazil. Int. J. Educ. Vocat. Guidance **20**(2), 351–373 (2019). https://doi.org/10.1007/s10775-019-09407-1
10. Rintala, H., Nokelainen, P.: Vocational education and learners' experienced workplace curriculum. Vocat. Learn. **13**(1), 113–130 (2019). https://doi.org/10.1007/s12186-019-09229-w

The Construction and Improvement of Digital Library Service

Cunling Liu[1] and Lindong Zhao[2(✉)]

[1] Shenzhen Institute of Information Technology, Guangdong 518172,
People's Republic of China
[2] Shenzhen Personnel and Talents Public Service Center, Guangdong 518172,
People's Republic of China

Abstract. In recent years, with the development of 5G information technology, big data, artificial intelligence and other communication technologies, the types and forms of information are becoming more and more rich, the functions of traditional libraries obviously cannot meet these needs. Therefore, the digital library is more and more familiar to people. this paper introduces the concept and development of digital books, the characteristics and types of digital libraries, analyzes the present situationof the development of digital libraries, emphatically puts forward the countermeasures that university libraries should take in the face of the development and change of digital books and paper books, and makes bold predictions for the development of digital libraries in the future.

Keywords: Digital books · Traditional library · Service

1 Introduction

Digital library is the product of high technology and information technology. The integration of information technology plays a very important role in the construction of digital library. Digital library mainly involves digital technology, super-large scale database technology, network technology, multimedia information processing technology, distributed processing technology, security and confidentiality technology, retrieval technology and mass information storage technology. However, as a new technology, there are still many unsolved problems in electronic library technology, especially in the field of university electronic library, there are still many aspects to be built and improved.

The application of digital library is developing along with the overall momentum of network publishing. Among them, Peking University Founder is the pioneer of online publishing in China. Teachers and students of Peking University can easily download digital books with copyright protection from the digital book channel of the library and use Apabi reading software for offline reading. With the continuous enhancement of China's economic strength and the continuous improvement of information level, e-books, online reading and other new ways of reading have been accepted and loved by more and more people. In the 21st century, with the enhancement of China's comprehensive national strength, university libraries, which have the functions of preserving

© Springer Nature Switzerland AG 2022
A. Katangur and L.-J. Zhang (Eds.): SCC 2021, LNCS 12995, pp. 84–90, 2022.
https://doi.org/10.1007/978-3-030-96566-2_7

human cultural heritage, developing information resources and participating in social education, have also been greatly developed, with a substantial increase in funding and a great improvement in infrastructure. At the same time, due to the rapid development of digital technologies such as scanning technology, storage technology, compression technology and the widespread popularity of the Internet, digital books, as an important tool of human civilization and culture transmission in the Internet era, they will play an increasingly important role. Digital libraries have the advantages of low cost, large storage capacity and convenient and fast retrieval. No matter in university libraries or public libraries, most of them have invested a lot of money to purchase e-books to enrich their collections. Take a university library in Shenzhen as an example. In recent years, the purchase funds of paper books and digital books are constantly changing. Among them, the purchase funds of digital books are increasing year by year (as shown in the figure below), and the growth rate is rapid. Digital books have become an important collection resource in university libraries.

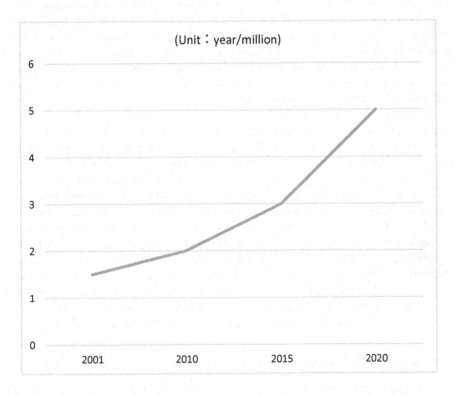

2 Current Situation and Problems

Compared with traditional paper books, digital books have many natural advantages, such as environmental protection, easy storage, short publishing cycle, large storage capacity, multimedia, easy retrieval, etc. At the same time, with the maturity of digital books technology, by the majority of readers love. However, digital books in the library is still a new thing, so there are various problems in the development process.

2.1 Insufficient Attention

Digital books in the library is a new thing, technology, standards and market is not perfect, people's reading habits are mainly paper books, digital books in the library is not enough attention. Although many libraries have purchased e-books, printed books still play an important role, and digital books are just one of the resources in their collections. Some are just "following the crowd". In this way, the quality of digital books is difficult to guarantee, and the utilization rate is certainly not too high.

2.2 Insufficient Funds

The function of a library is to collect, sort out, preserve and disseminate literature, and at the same time truly record and reflect the history of human beings' transformation of nature and society. Library is the crystallization of human civilization and the treasure house of human knowledge. Library has the functions of preserving human cultural heritage, developing social education, transmitting scientific information, developing intellectual resources and providing cultural entertainment, which has been widely valued and utilized by people since ancient times.

Nowadays, with the rapid development of science and technology, the position of library in the history of human development is more and more important. People regard books and materials as a kind of "national resources", which, together with materials and energy, are called the three pillars of science and technology. Mr. Ren Jiyu, the former director of the National Library of China, emphasized that "as a non-profit cultural facility for collecting, processing and storing all kinds of books, materials and information, libraries play an important role in the dissemination of knowledge and information, and are also the base of lifelong learning and education for the whole people. The library cannot be restricted by age and subject, and provide the required materials for readers to solve the lack of knowledge. Although libraries do not directly create wealth, they indirectly cultivate the people who create wealth. This is our contribution to society. Our educational functions are different from those of universities, with larger responsibilities, wider scope and deeper levels of service". Therefore, it is necessary to have enough funds as material support to realize the rapid development of university libraries.

2.3 Imperfect Technology

Digital books have come a long way, from the original single format to a variety of formats, such as PDF format, PDG format, NLC format, etc., from the original CD as the carrier of digital books to be able to read e-books, such as CD, disk, database, handheld e-book readers and other devices (smart phones, etc.) However, at present, there are no more than 20 kinds of domestic e-book formats, and there is not an executable national standard in reading software, and the software formats of major companies are incompatible with each other. If you buy e-books from more than one company, you have to install more than one reading software, which is very inconvenient for readers. In addition, the interface used to retrieve e-books is not uniform, and the retrieval of e-books must be entered into the corresponding retrieval interface. Some university libraries have purchased e-books from Springer, Jintu, Super Star, Founder, Shusheng and Meixing. Readers must enter six search pages if they want to look up e-books in the library. At the same time, six corresponding reading software must be installed, which brings great inconvenience to readers' access to e-books, and is undoubtedly a big obstacle to resource sharing. To a great extent, it hinders the circulation and use of e-books in the library.

2.4   The Content of Digital Book Resources is Uneven

With the development of e-book, technology and sales model are gradually mature. However, the content of e-book is not optimistic. It cannot keep up with the pace of the development of The Times and is far from meeting the needs of readers. Among the numerous e-book resources, literature and leisure resources account for the vast majority, while education and professional resources account for a small proportion (as shown in the figure below).

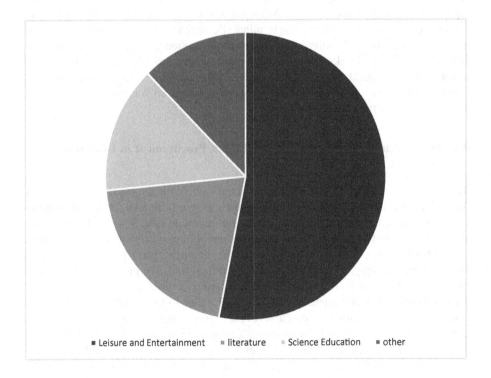

3   The Countermeasures

In recent years, the rapid development of digital books has made a great impact on the status of traditional libraries. Such as the concept of traditional library, facilities, document acquisition, cataloging, librarian quality, reader training, copyright protection, library evaluation, modern library management and so on. Although the development of digital books in China is rapid, it is still in the initial stage of development, the development of digital books themselves is not mature. Such as copyright, standard, price, network security and other issues, the traditional library in the introduction of digital books also need to solve these problems. Therefore, libraries should seek a complete scheme to actively deal with the challenge of digital books, so as to promote the promotion and popularization of e-books in libraries, and make electronic books and paper books mutually promote the development of libraries.

3.1   Enhance and Improve the Software and Hardware Environment of University Libraries

The traditional library needs a spacious and bright place for reading, while the e-book reading is different from paper books, which can only be finished with the help of certain equipment, PC or handheld reader. At the same time, it also requires high-speed and smooth network, fast running reading terminal (PC or reader), and library managers who are proficient in computer software development, operation and hardware maintenance. Before purchasing e-books, libraries must evaluate their existing equipment and staff to see if they can meet the needs of e-books. If the conditions do not meet, we must improve the library's hardware and software environment, so that electronic books can be integrated into the traditional library.

3.2   Strengthen the Perfection of Digital Book Procurement in University Libraries

The 21st century is an era of information explosion. With the rapid development of 5G technology, artificial intelligence, big data and so on, libraries, as the distribution center of information resources, are playing an important role. The good information service of library depends on the guarantee system of high-quality document resources. Digital book resources have gradually become an important part of library information resources and are playing a more and more important role. The procurement and input of digital books is the source of digital books entering the library. It is very important to do a good job in the procurement of digital books. Due to the differences in the types, nature and scale of libraries, the emphasis of purchasing e-books should be different. The content of digital books involves various disciplines and fields, and the content quality of e-books on the market is also different. Therefore, the selection of digital books has become complicated, involving a large number of disciplines and very complex majors. Therefore, it is necessary to purchase digital books scientifically according to the characteristics of the library itself, so as to achieve the balance between electronic resources and printing resources.

3.3 Ensure the Security and Stability of the Digital Book Service System

Different digital book providers have different technology advanced degree, so the service mode is also different. Therefore, college libraries should fully investigate and make prudent decisions to purchase safe and stable e-book service systems when purchasing e-books. Digital book suppliers and supply forms are diverse. The e-book resources provided by some suppliers are installed on the company's server, and the library only has remote access. Readers link through the library website, and finally read online or download encrypted e-books according to the permissions provided by the e-book suppliers. In fact, e-books purchased in this way are not substantial collections for the library, and there are certain risks. If the digital book provider's server fails, it will directly affect the library users' reading and downloading of e-books. If the contract expires or the company goes bankrupt, the library will lose the e-book resources and become nothing. The other way is that the library buys the e-book CD or database, loads the e-book data into the server of the library and runs it on the library network. Readers can read or download directly from the library website without transferring to the e-book seller's website. Moreover, these resources can become the library's permanent collection. This way of e-book service will be much more convenient for readers, and more secure and stable for libraries. It is also convenient for the statistics of download and page views and the timely understanding of the utilization rate of the resource. This way of e-book service has a very high requirement for the replacement of hardware and software environment in the library, and the library must provide sufficient guarantee from the aspects of equipment, network and database management personnel. Therefore, the library must closely combine its own hardware and software environment when purchasing e-books, and truly make the selected e-book service system suitable, which will not only save money, but also meet the needs of readers to the greatest extent.

3.4 Accelerate Talent Introduction and Training

Library is the crystallization of human civilization and the treasure house of human knowledge. It has the function of collecting, sorting out and storing documents, and plays a vital role in the development of the whole society. In today's information explosion, the traditional library should pay attention to the cultivation of talents, The library should not only have a good hardware environment, but also have the professional talents who master the computer technology, library information knowledge and information management knowledge, so the talent is the decisive factor. As a cultural and educational institution, the library stores and spreads the achievements of human knowledge, so it needs the compound talents with high cultural quality and broad knowledge to manage it. Qian Xuesen said, "Now the staff of libraries, archives and intelligence units should be information experts or information engineers, builders of information systems, guides and consultants for the use of (information)".

4 Conclusion

Facing the impact of digital resources such as e-books, databases and network resources on traditional libraries, traditional libraries in colleges and universities should actively respond to the challenges, constantly innovate ideas, accept new technologies, and promote the development of university libraries toward digitization and resource sharing. Improve the management level unceasingly, promote the computerization, intelligentization and automation of library work; Enhance and strengthen the service consciousness, advocate the service concept above readers, and accelerate the process of the globalization of service for readers and users. By introducing digital book resources into traditional libraries, on the one hand, the structure of library document resources can be optimized and the process of digitization and networking of library document resources can be accelerated; on the other hand, the document guarantee rate of library can be improved. At the same time, it can promote the inter-library cooperation and realize the sharing of information resources.

Acknowledgements. This research was supported by 2021 Annual Project of Shenzhen Institute of Information Technology (No. SZIIT2021SK006), "Eight Unified" College Ideological and Political Course Construction of demonstration site cultivation units.

References

1. Wu, J.: Prospect of Century Library. Shanghai Scientific and Technological Literature Publishing House, Shanghai (2000)
2. Niu, W.: Development status of digital library construction in China. Information Technology, 66–167 (2002)

Author Index

Printed in the United States
by Baker & Taylor Publisher Services